The

MANAGER'S
HANDBOOK

DAVID DODSON

The

MANAGER'S
HANDBOOK

FIVE SIMPLE STEPS
TO BUILD A TEAM, STAY FOCUSED, MAKE BETTER DECISIONS, AND CRUSH YOUR COMPETITION

WILEY

Published by John Wiley & Sons, Inc., Hoboken, New Jersey.
Published simultaneously in Canada.

Author note: Nothing in this book is intended to suggest legal advice for any situation or specific course of action. I am not a lawyer and am only conveying what I have come to understand through my own experience. The content in this book offers only general information and does not address how you might handle your specific situation, nor does it offer any guidance involving a particular set of facts or provide advice on how you might proceed, including any matters or situations involving legal matters or workplace violence. Nothing in this book implies an attorney–client relationship. The sample documents provide examples of my own experience, not legal advice, and are not a substitute for speaking with an attorney.

For general information on our other products and services or for technical support, please contact our Customer Care Department within the United States at (800) 762-2974, outside the United States at (317) 572-3993, or fax (317) 572-4002.

Wiley also publishes its books in a variety of electronic formats. Some content that appears in print may not be available in electronic formats. For more information about Wiley products, visit our web site at www.wiley.com.

Library of Congress Cataloging-in-Publication Data:

Names: Dodson, David M., author.
Title: The manager's handbook : five simple steps to build a team, stay focused, make better decisions, and crush your competition / David M. Dodson.
Description: Hoboken, New Jersey : Wiley, [2023] | Includes index.
Identifiers: LCCN 2023007774 (print) | LCCN 2023007775 (ebook) | ISBN
  9781394174072 (cloth) | ISBN 9781394174096 (adobe pdf) | ISBN
  9781394174089 (epub)
Subjects: LCSH: Management. | Leadership.
Classification: LCC HD31.2 .D637 2023 (print) | LCC HD31.2 (ebook) | DDC
  658—dc23/eng/20230421
LC record available at https://lccn.loc.gov/2023007774
LC ebook record available at https://lccn.loc.gov/2023007775

Cover Design: PAUL MCCARTHY
Cover Art: © SHUTTERSTOCK | IMAGEFLOW

SKY10096032_011025

Leaders aren't born, they are made. And they are made just like anything else, through hard work.

—Vince Lombardi

CONTENTS

FOREWORD
by H. Irving Grousbeck

We drink from wells we did not dig; we are warmed by fires we did not kindle.

—H. Irving Grousbeck, paraphrasing Deuteronomy 6:11

President John F. Kennedy, in an address shortly before his death in 1963, was discussing the then-current debate among scientists, and in Washington, about the feasibility of sending a human being to the moon. Kennedy cited a short story, written by the Irish author Frank O'Connor, one of his favorites. In that story, a young boy passed a high wall every afternoon on his way back from school. He gazed up at it each day, wishing he had the courage to climb it, so he could take a shortcut home. The afternoons, and the seasons, passed. Finally, one spring day as he neared the wall, he threw his cap over it. That commitment having been made, with great effort he succeeded in climbing the wall. Only with that mindset, concluded President Kennedy, would our country be able to reach the moon.

You've made the commitment to manage and lead, but that alone does not make you successful. That is what this book is for; to help you learn the necessary skills to succeed at managing. It is one thing to have the will to climb a wall, another to know how to do so.

As a professor, I'm often asked the following question: "Are entrepreneurs born, like .300 hitters in baseball are said to be, or can they be made?" My observation is that while the *desire* to lead may come from elsewhere, the *skills* required to lead are within one's ability to acquire. To be a successful manager you don't need to be impulsive, headstrong, bombastic, or flamboyant. If your life takes you down the path of leadership, there are no external barriers to success, only those you internally impose. If you want to master the skills of management quickly, the best shortcut is to follow the learnings and experiences of those who have come before you; what we often refer to as "best practices." If you learn only one thing from this book, it should be to not waste your precious and creative talents re-inventing what has already been discovered.

And as you master the management skills described in this book, also know that what you are doing is important. Leaders not only move an organization forward, they also affect individuals. Few from the next generation will remember the names of today's most prominent leaders. But the lives they touched are real. The most significant footprints that you leave will not be in the form of broad strategies, sweeping policies, or eloquent slide presentations at conventions. The grains of sand that matter are the instances you uplifted another. The times you served their career. It will be when you demonstrated morality and integrity, when doing so was inconvenient or expensive. Put more simply, where you manage well, you positively impact lives.

I say it's time to throw your cap over the wall, if you will. And in your journey toward mastering leadership, have a soft heart to go with your sharp mind, steadfastness of purpose, and Godspeed.

ACKNOWLEDGMENTS

The Manager's Handbook began almost five years ago as a single "whitepaper" on what to do during the first 100 days after buying a company. From there Susan Pohlmeyer and Hannah Dodson helped me write one whitepaper after another, until one day I thought we'd accidentally written a book. But I was wildly naïve. *The Manager's Handbook* only became possible after hundreds of hours on my part (I am so glad I did not track my time) and the wisdom and guidance from many people—so much so that there is no way I can remember them all, but let me try my best . . . .

I owe a debt to the community of chief executive officers and entrepreneurs I know who are running companies, who read various chapters of this book and provided me with invaluable insights, and to the tens of former students who were also kind enough to read early drafts and provide feedback for a final version. So many that I must thank them as one terrific group . . . thank you, all!

Jeff Stevens, Phil Rosenbloom, Jon Herzog, Kevin Taweel, Karen Liesching, and Graham Weihmiller each contributed generously and directly to the content of the work.

My colleagues at Stanford, to whom I owe so much learning about the best practices of management: Coley Andrews, Jennifer Dulski, Jim Ellis, Peter Kelly, Joel Peterson, and Gerald Risk. Graham Weaver was especially helpful in developing concepts of hiring and onboarding, frameworks for coachability, and the best way to use a hiring scorecard. There was also my mentor in writing and in discovering the balance between strategy and implementation, Michael Porter of Harvard Business School.

Simon Collins, Malcolm Collins, Chandos Mahon, Will Colt, and Laura Franklin provided detailed valuable feedback from the perspective of a new leader of an organization, and without their guidance we'd have missed the mark on how to present the learnings from *The Manager's Handbook*. Stephanie Cornell, Jamie Cornell, Linda Henry, and Dave Maney read early chapters and guided me with how best to position and structure the book.

Many great experts guided me on the key subskills. Lou Adler, the author of *Hire with Your Head*, was transformative in my development of a standardized hiring process that focused on *hiring for outcomes*. Stanford's former faculty member and author, Jim Collins, identified key data, and frameworks, for thinking about what makes for a great leader. Kim Scott's work on providing feedback was an excellent framework for my own development, and Cal Newport's development of Deep Work shaped much of my time-management practices that are described in the book. Much of what I learned regarding setting and adhering to priorities, especially KPIs, can be credited to my business partner John O'Connell.

Cam Lehman helped turn ideas into a readable book, as did Jan Alexander, my editor, and the guidance from Rick Wolff; and Richard Jacobs and David Aretha's copy edits. Kirstin Siegrist was the glue keeping the book, and my life, together. The folks at Wiley were sent from God: Sally Baker, Sheryl Nelson, Zach Schisgal, Deborah Schindlar, and Kezia Endsley came together as a team to transform a manuscript into a book. Tom Barbash was patient enough to teach me how to write, and while his work with me is unfinished, I owe any progress to him. This would not be a book if not for my agent Alice Martell, who first believed in this project, and then pushed me hard at every turn, and gratefully never let up on her commitment to excellence.

In my development as a manager, I want to thank my former board members: Jon Abbott, Jeff Bradach, Stephanie Cornell, Bill Egan, Gary Kusin, Bob Oster, Patty Ribakoff, Mitt Romney, Jim Southern, Richard Tadler, and Will Thorndike. In my development as a person, I owe the most to my three daughters: Rachel, Hannah, and Caroline.

To my wife Wendy, thank you for believing in me for things well beyond a single book and putting up with the dozen times I declared the book was complete.

And for everything else, Irv Grousbeck.

The

MANAGER'S
HANDBOOK

Introduction: Five Must-Have Skills from People Who Get Things Done

Vision without execution is daydreaming.

—Bill Gates

Despite earning an economics degree, working at McKinsey & Company, and then receiving an MBA from Stanford's elite business school, no one taught me the basic skills necessary to lead an organization. I had assumed that all of that prior experience had given me the tools to lead, but when I started my first company, I faced the not-so-pleasant reality that I'd never actually hired anyone, run a management meeting, or designed a compensation plan. Despite all the expensive business training, no one had taught me how to delegate effectively, let someone go, provide useful feedback, or create an annual operating plan—let alone how to do any of those things well. This was the work that now mattered. I discovered that credentials are not skills.

Instead, I learned on the job. Slowly and expensively. I made horrendous hiring mistakes, wasted cash, misused my team's time as well as my own. Along the way I lost great employees and valuable customers. Those missteps are the inspiration for this book.

Having now backed more than 100 entrepreneurs and taught several thousand MBA candidates, I know those early experiences of mine were not unique. There needed to be a better way to prepare people for leadership, and I became obsessed with the realization that the answer to great management lies not with the talent to see around corners, or by inventing the next big thing, but instead by learning to execute—put more simply, the ability to get things done.

My research also led to the rejection of the widespread theory that great leaders are born a certain way or can be defined by a distinctive set of personality traits. At the time of this writing, a Google search for "characteristics of entrepreneurs" generates well over 350 million results, most of which are platitudinous: *creative, passionate, motivated, resourceful,* or *dedicated.* These lists suggest that when it comes to leadership, you either are the right variety or you're not.

What we know is that there are enormous personality variations within the body of skilled entrepreneurs and leaders. Some are terrible public speakers, while others earn standing ovations. I know as many who present as introverts as extroverts. There are highly effective leaders who are bipolar. This increasingly diverse set of successful role models should forever bury any antiquated notion that management success should be limited to those who look a certain way.

Having rejected the "attribute theory" of entrepreneurial success, I became consumed with the nagging question that remained: Why are some people better than others at getting things done? After three years of observation and study, I discovered that what united all great managers was their mastery of a set of five common skills. Their personality attributes varied, but their command of these skills did not. It is universal. There are no exceptions. This was true for Dwight Eisenhower, Martin Luther King, Oprah Winfrey, and Bill Gates. This discovery excited me, principally because if the key to effective management is a set of skills, instead of attributes awarded at birth, the option of becoming an effective leader was open to almost anyone.

Whether it was sending rockets into space or drilling wells under the sea, exceptional managers shared five common skill characteristics that can be learned and applied by anyone—including you. These are the five skills universally shared by people who know how to get things done:

Skill 1: Commitment to Building a Team

Creating a great team is the reason why people with the same number of hours in the day, and days in the week, can manage organizations with thousands of employees. Former Stanford faculty member Jim Collins meticulously investigated the importance of building a team. Following five years of research he concluded:

> *Those who build great organizations make sure they have the right people on the bus and the right people in the key seats before they figure out where to drive the bus. They always think first about who and then about what.*[1]

Building such a team does not require superhuman abilities. It is about implementing a process that is nothing more complicated than implementing a series of well-established *skills*, all of which are described in this book and are virtually the same whether you are managing a single bookstore or building electric cars.

Skill 2: Fanatical Custodian of Time

Most of us waste much of our day, needlessly giving up valuable hours to pursuits that add little to no value to our organization. But freeing up more *quantity* of time alone is not enough. The creativity and insights that transform an organization seldom happen in slivers between answering emails and responding to routine requests. They require uninterrupted blocks of time, free from low-value transactional work. Managers who get things done never allow the priorities of others to interfere with what is important to them.

What we know, though, is that most time-management solutions require an extensive re-engineering of our habits and preferences, which is why they almost never stick. We understand that we need to change, and we make promises to do so, but always revert back to the prior bad habits. What is needed is a handful of modest adjustments that don't require any significant change to our existing routines, yet materially increase the *quantity* and *quality* of time we have.

Skill 3: Willingness to Seek and Take Advice

Management is not only about getting to the answer *quickly*; it's also about getting to the *right* answer. Making consistently good decisions outweighs any ego gratification that comes from being the source of all knowledge.

While most of the issues we face as managers have already been successfully met by others many times over, too many let their egos interfere with maximizing their potential. They worry that asking for counsel shows weakness. They may also fear being told that they might be wrong.

Yet the most confident leaders view things differently. To them, seeking and taking advice is a strategic weapon. They surround themselves with skillful advisors who have the experience, pattern recognition, and time to provide frank and direct advice—and they understand how best to utilize those advisors.

Skill 4: Setting and Adhering to Priorities

The temptation to overload the organization with competing priorities is titanic, leaving your team zigzagging among shifting initiatives while making little forward progress. Less experienced leaders get frustrated, wondering why those around them "can't move fast enough," forgetting that implementing those great ideas of yours requires hiring people, buying equipment, designing marketing material, building control systems, and leasing space—all of which takes time.

Steve Jobs once told an audience at the Apple Worldwide Developer's Conference, "You've got to say 'no, no, no' and when you say 'no,' you piss off people." He understood that ideation is faster than implementation. To be successful, even in a company with resources as vast as Apple's, one can only accomplish a small list of things very well.

Skill 5: An Obsession with Quality

Ask yourself this simple question: Which do you fear more, a competitor that has a better sales team or one that has a better product? Of course, it's a superior product or service that you worry most about. In today's world of instant communication, customers know who the most reliable person is to mow their lawn, which big-screen TV is the best on the market, and which software solution is most reliable. Organizations can't hide from today's information vortex—and those that provide great quality don't want to.

Quality is not about virtue but about making money. It's the easiest and most sustainable way to increase profit because quality drives revenue, improves your pricing power, and lowers your expenses. Providing terrific quality, though, is not about slogans or mission statements. It requires a set of skills to accurately assess what your customer wants and needs, knowing how to implement those features throughout your organization, and then using leading indicators to make the right operational decisions.

Having identified these five skills shared among people who know how to get things done, I had no interest in writing yet another business book that strafed at 10,000 feet, dropping soundbites and theories, leaving the reader momentarily inspired but without knowing what to do next. I wanted to write a how-to manual that would help the tens of thousands of everyday leaders and managers who want to be better at getting things done.

This challenge led me to consider how our minds master other skills, such as playing the piano, artistic painting, or golf. I realized that we master these skills by learning a set of *subskills* that combine to master the *primary skill*. For instance, in learning to play the piano, you need to know how to read music, how to position your fingers across the keyboard while navigating 88 black and white keys, and the difference between a sharp and a flat. It is the mastery of these subskills, each within most people's ability, that represent the difference between playing "Chopsticks" and Paul McCartney's "Let It Be." In the same way, this book breaks each of the five skills into a set of easily accessible subskills. Learn the subskills, and you master the primary skill.

My last challenge was how to present material in a way that a busy reader could quickly, easily, and effectively master. Not so long ago, the *Harvard Business Review* sent me a 241-page piece on the subskill of running a good management meeting. My bookcase has dozens of books discussing just the subskill of hiring. All of this material is good, but few of us have the time to read thousands of pages to get a few dozen pages of actionable content. I should know—I remember in my early days as an entrepreneur when I barely had time for meals.

My aim was not to fill pages in a book for you to slog through, but to get you the vital information in the most efficient way possible. Which is why I explain each subskill in as *few* words as possible, as *plainly* as possible, and end each chapter with a short summary of the material, which becomes your battle plan for implementation. This explains why some chapters are longer than others. I had no desire to create cookie cutter chapters to fit into a book, because I know that you don't have time for that. *The Manager's Handbook* is a book to use, not just to read. It is the book I wished someone had handed me when I first became a manager.

This is the unique insight of *The Manager's Handbook:* identify the primary skills necessary to run something; break them down into a combined set of subskills that can be mastered by just about anyone; and present them in a format designed for busy people.

At that point I thought my work was complete. That was until the afternoon I was talking with my friend, Professor Michael Porter, who had completed reading a draft. He said in a certain way that I was thinking about it all wrong. Michael Porter is the author of 19 books on leadership, including the seminal piece on strategy, *Competitive Strategy. Fortune* magazine said of Professor Porter, "He has influenced more executives than any other business professor on earth," so I knew to pay attention.

Michael told me that I had incorrectly reduced the five skills to a checklist. To have a chance at greatness, one has to recognize that they function as a set of united subskills. To make his point he listed off a handful of subskills from the book, and how they interrelate: that in order to create an effective *operating plan,* one needs to have identified the *key performance indicators* that drive the business. And to do that, an effective manager would have *built a team*, which would require mastering the skills of *hiring, onboarding*, and *delegation*. That same leader would need to manage against that *operating plan* implemented through *effective meetings*, and vetted with their *mentors and advisors*.

His point was that the five skills of people who know how to get things done represent a unifying principle for execution. He told me, "Understanding the competitive landscape is essential, but simply the desire to do things is not enough. The best strategy won't lead to success if a leader can't implement it effectively." Which is why he then said to me that these five skills should not serve as options to be selectively ordered off a menu, but instead were most powerful when implemented in combination with one another. The risk was that my readers would pick and choose the easiest skills and look past the others. Professor Porter saw that I'd created not a list of things, but a unifying theory of execution.

Whether you are an entrepreneur leading your own show, a manager running a department within an established organization, or a middle-school principal, this is a how-to manual for people serious about getting things done.

———————————

I want to now leave you with the story of Roy Halladay and the day he pitched a perfect game on May 29, 2010. A perfect game means no batters made it to base during all nine innings: 27 batters up, and 27 sent to the dugout. A perfect game is no small achievement. Since 1880, only 23 perfect games have been pitched, and no major league pitcher has been able to do it more than once in his career.

What struck me about the story I read was not what Halladay accomplished that day on the pitcher's mound, but what his coach said to him as the two of them walked across the outfield before the game. Rich Dubee told Halladay, "Go out there and try to be good. If you go out there and try to be good, you've got a chance to be great."

PART I
Commitment to Building a Team

1 Hire for Outcomes

If you want to go fast, go alone. If you want to go far, go together.

—African proverb

Apple, Inc. didn't invent the mouse, the graphic interface, or even the personal computer, but it turned these technologies into one of the most valuable companies in the world because Steve Jobs was ruthless about surrounding himself with top talent. His leadership is one of the best examples of "First Who, Then What," the expression coined by the business expert Jim Collins, in *Good to Great*.[1] Jobs understood that inventing the next *big thing* wouldn't make a lick of difference if he didn't have the right team in place to pull it off. "No one can whistle a symphony. It takes an orchestra to play it," as Halford E. Luccock, the early twentieth-century Methodist minister, once said.

Yet most managers are really bad at hiring. A study involving 7,000 hiring managers found that 46% of all new hires fail within the first 18 months, and a mere 19% achieved "unequivocal success."[2] Can you imagine accepting those results in any other aspect of your business? Instead of hiring for outcomes—or put more bluntly, hiring "to get things done"— most of us hire the person whom we personally click with, cross the chore off our to-do list, and willingly accept a 50/50 shot at having gotten it right.

Fortunately, hiring for outcomes doesn't require special instincts or talents. Better hiring begins with committing to a standardized approach across your organization. Standardizing your process eliminates the risk that someone will follow an incorrect approach, anchors the team to best practices, and allows for process improvement—which can take place only by iterating on a common process.[3]

The conventional objection to standardization is that it takes away the hiring manager's flexibility. But a process of hiring for outcomes does not impact anyone's role in exercising their judgment in making a final decision; it increases the quality of the data collected in order to improve the eventual decision.

Hiring for outcomes works. When an international nonprofit I cofounded, Sanku LLC, hired three country directors in a row who did not last, I pressed the organization to implement the steps outlined in this chapter. All seven of their next country directors were successes. Today, Sanku is providing fortified foods to millions of at-risk families, but only because of their top-notch team.

Focus on Outcomes, Not Intuition

In the book *Talking to Strangers,* Malcolm Gladwell describes a world leader who flew to meet with a foreign counterpart in order to size him up. Similar to how most of us interview candidates for a job, the prime minister wanted to look into the other person's eyes, watch his body language, and decide whether he could be trusted in an important global matter.[4] Upon returning from his meeting, British Prime Minister Neville Chamberlin said of the German chancellor:

> *He gave me the double handshake that he reserves for special friendly demonstrations . . . I had established a certain confidence which was my aim . . . I saw in his face the impression that here was a man who could be relied upon when he had given his word.*

Chamberlin recklessly relied on gut feel and likeability over data. "The people who were wrong about Hitler were the ones who had talked with him for hours," writes Gladwell, describing Hitler's ability to connect to others personally. Because many of the people who should be experts at evaluating others substitute gut feel for data and process, "We have . . . CIA officers who cannot make sense of their spies," Gladwell writes, "judges who cannot make sense of their defendants, and prime ministers who cannot make sense of their adversaries." Winston Churchill, who never met Hitler, drew the *correct* conclusion, in large part because his judgment was based on observations of the chancellor's actions, and not influenced by his demeanor. Based on the data, Churchill correctly pronounced him "a monster of wickedness, insatiable in his lust for blood and plunder."

You need not look beyond your own hiring record to see the case for a process that focuses on outcomes. We never hear someone saying they want to promote an internal candidate because they "like" the person or because the person graduated from Princeton—certainly not because of the way they shake your hand. Which is why hiring internal candidates, versus those less known to the organization, has a 20% greater success rate than hiring from outside the organization.[5] The disparity happens because we promote internal candidates based on their *past performance*, recognizing that past performance is the best single indicator of *future performance*—what the hiring expert Lou Adler calls "hiring with your head." Internal candidates are promoted because we believe they will produce desired outcomes.

Create a Hiring Scorecard

I was once asked to assist in hiring an operations manager for a trucking and transportation business. In one resume, a candidate spelled the word *referral* with only one "r." A member of the team suggested that we not interview the person. The misspelling was evidence of poor attention to detail. But we weren't hiring a copy editor or English teacher. We were looking for someone who could direct a fleet of trucks, improve gross margin by 5%, and lead a blue-collar workforce. I challenged the team on whether we'd be okay with an awful speller if the operations manager could do those three things exceedingly well. As you can guess, we hired the bad speller. He brought a seven-point gross margin improvement to the bottom line within a year—and with those results, no one ever complained that he continued to be a lousy speller.

Hiring without a scorecard is like shooting an arrow, then justifying your decision by drawing the bullseye around wherever the arrow lands. Instead, begin by defining the desired *outcomes* without regard to the person's prior experience. In hiring a vice president of sales, you're not looking for someone with an MBA or 10 years of sales experience. You're looking for a person who can increase revenue. That's the difference between experience and outcomes. Experience is what they did in the past; outcomes are what they will do for you if you hire them. When my friend Paul English, a founder of several successful companies, including the travel business Kayak, wanted to disrupt the travel industry he specifically avoided hiring anyone with travel experience because that experience had nothing in common with the outcomes he sought.

With this goal, you won't be afraid to hire someone who is making a stretch in responsibility just because they have not done the same job before. Actually, you'll tend to favor those with less conventional experience. To again quote from Lou Adler:

> To me, the worst is to hire people with the same type of experience in the same type of job in the same industry. While this is easy to do and logically comfortable, you'll continually under-hire. People who are willing to do the same old things repeatedly are just cruising along. They aren't top performers.[6]

While the concept of a hiring scorecard is not new, I like the framework that my colleague Graham Weaver developed, which begins with a list of desired outcomes. Let's use the example of a vice president of sales. Such a scorecard might begin like this (Figure 1.1):

Outcomes
Grow revenue from $30 to $50mm in 2 years
Increase client additions from 20 to 70 in 1 year
Grow sales team from 4 to 7
Build culture of creativity and accountability

Figure 1.1 Hiring Scorecard—Outcomes

Next, you'll need to answer the question: "How will I know?" This becomes your hiring action plan, allowing you to target the data you need to collect (Figure 1.2).

Outcomes	How will I know?
Grow revenue from $30 to $50mm in 2 years	Track record hitting sales targets
Increase client additions from 20 to 70 in 1 year	Experience successfully scaling
Grow sales team from 4 to 7	Track record of hiring/training
Build culture of creativity and accountability	Managed sales team and hit quotas

Figure 1.2 Hiring Scorecard—Outcomes

But outcomes per se are not enough. To finish your scorecard, you need to identify the right *attributes*, which are the reason someone is likely to achieve the outcome (Figure 1.3). Attributes are not proficiencies like using PowerPoint or operating a backhoe. They are the qualities, characteristics, and traits of a person. To build a correct set of these attributes, use this simple trick. Identify people who have succeeded at your company in similar positions. Then list the attributes that are common among them.

Attributes	How will I know?
Emotional intelligence	Self-awareness during interview
Humility	Discussion of successes and failures
Continual learner	Investing in him/herself
Will to win	Record of hitting sales quotas and goals
Strong leader	Attracting A-players

Figure 1.3 Hiring Scorecard—Attributes

The reason to emphasize attributes over skills is the simple reason: attributes tend to be hardwired into our nature, skills can be taught. Ray Dalio, who built one of the greatest investment teams in history, says, "Weigh values and abilities [aka, "attributes"] more heavily than skills in determining whom to hire."

There is no magic number, but generally avoid listing more than five attributes or outcomes. While we often find comfort in long lists, a process that evaluates dozens of attributes and outcomes is impractical to manage, and inevitably we drift away from testing for the "must-have" qualities and retreat back to substituting gut feel and instinct over an accurate hiring process.

Use a Team Approach

In the ancient Eastern fable, a group of blind villagers comes across a strange animal. Each of them touches a different part of the animal (Figure 1.4). Because they have their own set of facts, they arrive at different conclusions. Touching the trunk, one suggests the animal is like a snake; another who touches the leg believes the animal resembles a tree.

Figure 1.4 Touching the Elephant

The same is true when people conduct interviews by themselves and meet afterward to discuss what they learned. Since the interviewers each asked their own questions and heard a unique set of responses, like the villagers in the fable, the interpretation of that information is shared through the prism of their individual data sets.

This way of interviewing also commonly gives an outsized voice to the most senior person, or whoever is the most persuasive or forceful. Candice might say, "I found Larry showed a lack of humility when he talked about the department's achievements," and Sauda then accepts the judgment of her senior colleague even though she'd come to a different conclusion, which she drew from a different set of data. Sauda must defer to Candice as there is no way to reconcile Candice's and Sauda's differing views because they are based on each having touched a different part of the elephant.

Team interviewing also allows for better listening. When we interview one-on-one, a portion of our attention has to be focused on crafting the next question or managing the candidate's response. That inevitably impacts the degree to which we can listen and observe. But during a team interview, while one team member asks questions, the others can study the person without those distractions.

Yet conducted improperly, team interviewing can resemble an out-of-control press conference—with everyone firing off questions at the candidate—limiting the quality of the data collected and, in parallel, overwhelming the person being interviewed with unrelated questions being thrown at them. To avoid this, designate one person as the *primary*, who will do most of the questioning on behalf of the team. Then, before moving to the next line of questioning, the primary should invite others to ask any questions so that everyone has a chance to ask any questions they may have. In this way, no one feels the need to interrupt or prematurely shift the line of questioning in a new direction.

The team approach also allows for a faster process. Instead of asking the candidate an identical question three times, when you interview the candidate as a team, you truncate the process in about half the time. In today's market, this is a recruiting weapon as speed can often be the deciding factor in landing a great hire.

Finally, make clear that while everyone on the team gets a voice, not everyone necessarily receives a vote. Establish up front how the final decision will be made so that all of those participating understand their role, and they don't mistake their participation and influence for having hiring authority.

Systematic Interviewing

Early in my career, I had a favorite interview question: *How do you know if the light goes out when you close the refrigerator door?* At the time, I told myself that it helped me measure the candidate's creativity. But my question failed to provide any useful data that would help me measure a person's ability to achieve any of the desired outcomes I was hiring against. Truth be told, I was just showing off with a clever riddle. Worse than adding no value, enchanted by an ingenious response to my brainteaser, I'd find myself impressed, which undoubtedly opened me to biases like Hitler's handshake. Over time, I learned to discard all my crafty questions and resorted to three systematic interview steps.

Step 1: Understand the Resume

Review the resume in chronological order, beginning as early as grade school. Most high performers demonstrate important attributes early in life. These might come in the form of after-school jobs, extracurricular activities, or awards. This information also provides a context for the arc of their life. The starting line is not the same for all of us. Understanding that a candidate's parent lost his or her job, and the candidate worked after school to help the family financially, may disclose a valuable attribute. Similarly, a fourth-generation Yale University legacy, who grew up comfortably in Greenwich, Connecticut, may be less impressive than a candidate who had to work nights for the tuition money to graduate from a land grant college.

If state laws allow, get salary or wage information as far back as possible.[7] If someone consistently received compensation increases, that is evidence of high accomplishment. While there are biases when it comes to compensation, a consistent pattern of upward pay remains a reliable indicator of an individual's value to an organization. But don't jump to assumptions. If you see a flat or downward pattern in compensation, ask for clarification. You might otherwise miss that the candidate took a pay cut to move closer to a specialty program for an ill child, or as a trade-off to participate in a stock equity program.

To understand any resume gaps, ask for the month of each job change. If the prospective employee doesn't know the specific months, ask for the time between the departure from one job and the start of the next. If they deflect with something along the lines of, "I wanted to take some time off and be with my family," you'll need to be willing to follow up with a question such as: "What was the motivation for taking time off at that particular time?" The answer could be evidence of being asked to resign or the choice to thoughtfully reflect on their career before taking the next job. You won't know if you're not willing to ask.

For more recent jobs, draw the organization chart with the candidate's current position and, if applicable, the previous position. Get the names of supervisors and subordinates, which will be the basis for your subsequent reference checks. Note each person's name, ask for the proper spelling, and then ask how to reach them. This makes it clear that you plan to talk with these people, sometimes called TORC (threat of reference check). TORC alone often reduces any exaggerations, embellishments, or excessive boasting during the interview. The best candidates—the ones you want on your bus— will welcome you speaking with those they've worked with, and to the extent there are issues of confidentiality, assure them that you will sort that out with them prior to contacting anyone.

As you draw the organization chart, record the revenue or budget for each department they worked in or managed. This provides context for later questions, and for whether the candidate's scope of responsibility increased or decreased over time. When hiring people who will be managing a department and building a team, find out who they hired, who they inherited, and how many people they had to replace and why. Then ask them to rank their subordinates. This information will be a treasure in subsequent interviews, where you will be able to ask such questions as: *Why did you let this person go? What were the characteristics that led you to hire this person? Why, if this person is rated a C, did you keep them for 17 months?*

Resist the temptation to form an opinion as you review their resume. Later in the process, you don't want to get anchored to an earlier opinion and fall prey to *confirmation bias*, where you are predisposed to focus on the evidence that supports your initial conclusion.

Step 2: Deepening and Narrowing

Deepening and narrowing begins with asking the candidate for examples of situations that may be indicative of future performance. By avoiding hypothetical situations or generalities, such as *"How do you like to manage people?"* (where the candidate's response is often their best guess at what you want to hear), you'll focus on actual past behavior and use that data to predict their ability to achieve future outcomes.

Let's look at a typical interview exchange:

Q: *What led you to do so well at Sentech Software?*

A: *I'm good at motivating people to reach their highest potential. Good management is about having the best people and then letting them perform to their utmost potential.*

Many interviewers stop there and move on, especially if the candidate delivered the answer with polish. But this response has taught us nothing except that the person had a practiced answer to a predictable question. Instead, follow up with deepening and narrowing. Smart and Street, the authors of *Who: The A Method for Hiring*, developed a simple framework to guide the process of deepening and narrowing, which they call: *"What? How? Tell me more."*[8] Here's an example of using this framework:

Q: <u>*What*</u> *is an example of when you motivated a particular person that meets that description, and how did those actions increase their potential?*

A: *Last year I inherited the customer success team. They were discouraged with our low rankings and our turnover was high. I fixed that.*

Q: <u>*How*</u> *specifically did you fix that?*

A: *I designed a new bonus plan that the company implemented. I also had weekly success meetings, where we celebrated the wins and troubleshot the problems.*

Q: <u>*Tell me more.*</u> *Did it work?*

A: *Our quality score went from negative 21 to positive 37, and our turnover in the department dropped from 70% to almost zero.*

Notice how much we learned by asking only three structured questions. Deepening and narrowing also reveals when a boast doesn't hold up. For instance:

Q: _What_ is an example of where you used your competitiveness to the company's advantage?

A: _I fight to hit my quarterly numbers. I'm as competitive as any person about my targets._

Q: _How_ did you accomplish this?

A: _Three quarters ago we were close to missing plan, and I held several contests. Sure enough, we made our goal._

Q: _Tell me more._ What contests did you hold that quarter that you did not hold in the prior quarter?

A: _We ran the standard company contest. We weren't allowed to make changes unless it was consistent with what corporate designed._

Using deepening and narrowing, we learn that the boast ("I'm as competitive as any person about my targets") was based on implementing standard company programs.

Smart and Street also suggest measuring results along three benchmarks: _previous, plan,_ and _peers._ Using this framework, if someone were to tell you that they sold $1.2 million in revenue, you would then ask what the revenue was in the _previous_ two years, how that compared with the organization's _plan,_ and how they did in comparison to their _peers._

Beware that during the deepening and narrowing, the interview can be bogged down when the interviewee offers stories often unconnected to your question. You'll need to politely keep them focused on your line of questioning. If you're unwilling to interrupt them and maintain your focus, you'll never collect the necessary data in any reasonable time frame. For example, you may try saying:

> _I'm excited to get to know you as well as possible, and I want you to have time to ask me questions. If I ever interrupt you, it's with those goals in mind._

Freely move to the next topic once you have clarity on the outcome or attribute you're investigating. If one attribute was the ability to hire well, and in your first five minutes you learned they follow a rigorous hiring process, reduced turnover by half, and several of their hires went on to be promoted, use the extra time to move to other attributes that may take longer to evaluate rather than consume time on an issue you've already reached clarity on.

Step 3: Caucus with the Team

Left with about 20 minutes, let candidates know that you're adjourning for a short caucus to determine if there are questions that have not yet been covered. In the caucus, do not poll the team on whether they "like the candidate," and avoid any discussion that borders on reaching conclusions. You are caucusing strictly to identify any areas that require further questioning before the candidate leaves.

With the scorecard in hand, ask each member of the interview team if they have any open areas of interest or have spotted any ambiguities or concerns in which to collect more data. For example, if someone raises a concern that a candidate may be too harsh on his or her staff, you might return with questions about turnover, the last few terminations the candidate was involved with, and any experience with performance reviews.

When you do so, make sure to allow candidates time to ask you questions. This is a matching exercise, and they need to do their own diligence on you. As well, you'll learn more about them as you note what they asked, what they care about, and their level of preparation.

Following each interview, reconvene to review the data you collected and compare it against your scorecard. It is important that the interview team talk about each candidate immediately following the interview. Notes are imperfect, and memories fade quickly. As you discuss what you learned, avoid making what seems like a hiring opinion—the decision at hand is only whether to take the next step in the hiring process, not to decide who you want to hire. This mindset helps prevent anchoring on a position that will later impact your objectivity. If a member of your team makes statements such as "I really like her," or "He's my front runner," reset the conversation to determining only if a candidate shows sufficient evidence of likely outcomes and attributes to have them back for more questions. You are collecting data, not drawing conclusions. As you determine whether you want to continue with a candidate, while the information is fresh, write down what you want to accomplish in further interviews.

Further Interviews

The next interviews will follow the same structure: a primary questioner, team members who have a chance to ask questions at certain points, adherence to the scorecard, deepening and narrowing, a preliminary caucus, additional questions, time for candidates to ask you questions, and a final caucus.

Before further interviews, the team should review their notes from the earlier interview, agree on what needs clarification, and decide how you'll resolve any open issues or concerns. In these interviews, don't follow an identical approach with every candidate. This is your chance to dig deeper into specific areas of interest. For example, if Akio seemed to have higher emotional intelligence than Curtis, but you're uncertain, in the next interview you would spend more time asking Curtis questions that will lead to clarity around his emotional intelligence.

Consider selectively providing candidates with questions in advance. Most interviewing over-emphasizes the ability to think fast on one's feet, but that is not a skill used often in work settings. You don't want to favor a quick thinker over a more thoughtful person who may drive better outcomes. With prepared questions, you'll also be able to assess the extent of their preparation: one candidate may show up with notes and work-product examples in response to the questions you sent in advance, while another may answer on-the-fly.

To help formulate your offer and to convince the person to join your organization, be sure to find out where you stand competitively. Consider asking questions along these lines:

How would you react if you gave notice to your current employer, and they offered you more money to stay?

Are you conducting a full-scale job hunt or being selective and opportunistic?

What other offers do you have in-hand or are you anticipating?

How does this position compare to those?

Why are you interested in this position?

No job is perfect, so if you could change any part of this job, what would it be?

Having completed several interviews, have the team answer a simple question: "If I were hiring in advance of need instead of filling a vacancy, would I hire this person, or would I wait and see more candidates?" Then open the conversation up to general observations.

If you are not sure of your conclusion, decide whether to invite the candidate back for yet another interview, or consider the option of a short phone call to clear up those areas of uncertainty. Do not give up on a candidate solely because you are on the fence. In most cases, you are on the fence because you need more data.

Reference Checks

Years ago, I needed a senior executive during a critical time in my company's geographic expansion. When I met one candidate, let's call him Vincent, I was certain after only 20 minutes that he was perfect for the job. During our caucus, we considered making him an offer on the spot. At that point in my career, I had hired a dozen senior managers, and I had confidence in my instincts. Enough so that even though Vincent had previously worked for a company whose president I knew, I didn't see any reason to bother with a reference check. I wanted to hire Vincent before someone else got to him first. You of course know where this is headed. Vincent did not work out. It turned out that he lacked many of the attributes that were on my scorecard, and in his earlier positions had not demonstrated an ability to achieve the critical outcomes of the job I was hiring for. The hardest part of this story to admit is that I later ran into that friend of mine. After I told him what happened he said, "Why didn't you call? I could have told you not to hire Vincent."

You cannot make a good hiring decision without checking references. There is only so much precision you can expect from the interviewing process, and the reference check is often your richest source of data. There is no better judge of a person's match against your scorecard than someone who directly witnessed their work.

A common mistake, though, is to save the reference check until the end of the process, right before making an offer. At that stage you're again highly susceptible to confirmation bias. A Stanford University study revealed that confirmation bias is most prevalent when three circumstances are present: the consequences of being wrong are high, the decision-maker has a large investment in the decision, and the issue is emotional. All three of these conditions are present at the end of a demanding interview process, which means you're predisposed to hear what you want to hear. To quote from *Hire with Your Head*:

> *You can get any answer you want from a reference check. If you don't have an open mind and are not willing to change your opinion, it's a waste of time even to contact the reference.*[9]

Furthermore we generally get the answer we want due to the *observer-expectancy effect*, the cognitive bias when we unknowingly rig the questions to get the results we want. For example, you might ask:

> *We're looking at hiring Charlotte for vice president of operations. We think she's terrific, but I want to make sure you don't know anything that would make us not want to hire her. Any big red flags we need to know about?*

By asking the question in this way, I maximize the chances of getting the result I want, which is to hear nothing that might disrupt my plan to hire Charlotte. At this point I'm not collecting data. I'm praying for confirmation, reminding me of what the author John Steinbeck once said, "No one wants advice. Only corroboration."

The best defense against the observer-expectancy effect is to complete your reference checks when you're still deciding *among* candidates. If you're struggling to decide which candidate to hire, you invite critical feedback because you're not looking to confirm a candidate, but to eliminate candidates. In this way you'll ask the hard questions because you're searching for data to help you with the decision of who to *eliminate*.

Because most people don't want to negatively impact someone's chance at a new job, create the best environment for the reference to be objective and analytical. To make it easier for the person to be critical, position the conversation away from whether the person is capable and accomplished, and certainly whether they are a good person, and make it about identifying for them the best next career move:

> *We're enthusiastic about Jing-Yu. I'm hoping to explore fit. Jing-Yu is more than capable of doing a terrific job, but since neither of us would be doing her a favor by steering her into the wrong job, on a confidential basis can I ask you some questions?*

You'll need to follow up with the same rigor you used in your interviewing process—employing the techniques of *deepening and narrowing*; *what, how, tell me more*; and *previous, plan,* and *peers*. While you will be more diplomatic with a person's reference, just like in your interviews with the candidates, don't let references off the hook with generalities and hypotheticals. Those are no more useful from a reference than they are from the candidate.

Be Nice

In today's world, where online information flows instantaneously, it is even more critical to treat all candidates with civility and professionalism—even those you pass on. I was recently told a story by a college graduate who made it to the final round of a process. In the interview, the manager showed up 20 minutes late and glanced at his email as the graduate spoke. The next day, the graduate posted about the experience on Glassdoor to warn others. My friend Paul English instructs his team:

> *Do not ever be late, even by two minutes. Do not ever take any interruptions, even if you get a phone call from the President of the United States. Show the candidate that you came into work to meet with them, that they are the most important person on your list.*

To Paul, hiring well means an all-hands-on-deck approach:

> *Ask the visitor if they want a soda or drink. Do not ever leave a job candidate sitting on a couch waiting for someone. If you see someone sitting alone (bored),*

energize them by saying hello and chatting with them. It could mean the difference in winning over that superstar candidate, and having ALL candidates speak highly of their experience with us.

A Final Thought . . .

There is often a trade-off to make between people with lots of *experience* who can hit the job running versus less experienced people with the *attributes* that will make them a better long-term hire. Graham Weaver introduced me to a simple framework for evaluating this trade-off (Figure 1.5).

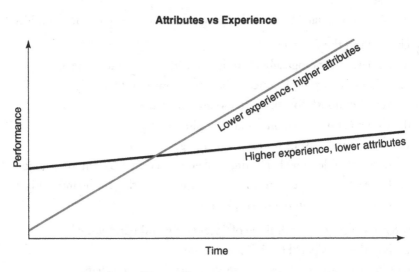

Figure 1.5 Attributes Versus Experience

Depending upon the situation, those two lines may cross in a few months or a few years. Graham's point is not that there is a single right answer. The point is to shift evaluating the trade-off from an abstract concept to a specific time frame. Draw the lines with your best estimate of when those two lines cross. It won't be perfect, but it will be far better than any conceptual notion circulating in your head. Armed with your supposition, you'll be certain to make a better decision on what to do in your particular situation.

Hire for Outcomes

1. Hire based on data, not instinct, intuition, likability, or gut feel.

2. Hire against a scorecard that lists the desired *outcomes* and the required *attributes*, then create a strategy for "*How will I know?*"

3. Hiring is a team sport.

4. Establish a process:
   a. Interview together to create a single data set.
   b. For an orderly process, designate a "primary" questioner.
   c. Caucus before the candidate leaves and identify any areas requiring clarification.
   d. Meet immediately after each interview, focusing on data, not likability.

5. Understand the resume:
   a. Review chronologically to understand the arc of their career.
   b. Ask about accomplishments, beginning early in their life.
   c. Get the month for the start and end of each job.
   d. Understand the reason for any employment gaps.
   e. Discuss the reasons for each job change.
   f. If permissible, note beginning and ending compensation for each job.
   g. For each area of responsibility, note the size of the candidate's budget, revenue, and number of employees.

6. Interview using the technique of "deepening and narrowing:"
   a. Ask them: What? How? Tell me more.
   b. Compare accomplishments to Previous, Peers, and Plan.
   c. Remember: "Past performance is the best single indicator of future performance."

7. Consider providing questions in advance of the interview that benefit from prior reflection and preparation.

8. Check references:
   a. For the two most recent positions, draw an organization chart with names and contact information.
   b. Conduct reference checks when you are choosing *among* candidates, not *confirming* your choice.

9. Be nice.

Ten Initial Interview Questions to Ask

1. You strike me as a competitive person. Can you give me an example of when you used your competitiveness to the company's advantage?

2. Can you give me an example of when you were criticized for something and that criticism was justified?

3. What about an example of when you were criticized unfairly?

4. Can you give me an example of where [an aspect of their personality] hurt your work?

5. Describe a situation when you failed to reach a goal.

6. You said you look for [stated qualities] when you hire people. Can you tell me specifically what questions you ask a candidate to identify those qualities?

7. How many people were you directly involved in hiring in the last two years, and how many of those would you consider to be A-players today?

8. Please describe an example of a hiring mistake you made, what you learned, and then what you changed about your hiring process?

9. Let's assume you were giving yourself a performance review, careful to be specific and actionable about your suggestions. What would be your two most important developmental challenges going into the next year?

10. Do you have any questions for me?

Ten Questions to Give the Candidate in Advance*

1. What did you do over the last year that makes you the proudest?

2. If you could, what would you change about your current position?

3. Describe a time when you were totally committed to a task.

4. We'd like to accomplish [objective] during the next year. Tell me about your most significant related accomplishment.

5. Tell me something about yourself that is not on your resume that you'd like me to know about you.

---

*Questions that lend themselves to reflection and preparation.

6. Describe a time when you disagreed with a decision that was made at work.

7. Please bring in an example of a [presentation, writing sample] that you are particularly proud of, which you completed in the last six months. Be sure to block out any confidential information.

8. Describe a professional situation you faced that you would never want to face again.

9. What could your current company do to be more successful?

10. Who has been your favorite boss so far, and why did you choose him or her?

Ten Questions to Ask a Reference

1. What role did you play in the organization and how did the two of you interact?

2. How did [candidate] rank among his/her peers?

3. What did she/he do differently than her/his peers to achieve that ranking? Can you offer an example of the candidate doing that?

4. Let's assume you're reviewing [candidate] in an annual review. What would be the two most important developmental opportunities for her/him?

5. Can you give me an example of how these developmental opportunities affected his/her performance?

6. What types of work environments does the candidate work best in? For example, I do the best at [personal example].

7. How was [candidate] measured, and how did she/he perform against those targets/budget?

8. [After an answer to questions 2 and 7 is provided] What keeps this candidate from being at the very top? Can you give an example?

9. How did the candidate's performance in his/her last year compare to the prior year?

10. What did she/he do to contribute to the [company performance] from the prior year?

2 The 100-Day Window

The greatest leader is not necessarily the one who does the greatest things. He is the one that gets the people to do the greatest things.

—Ronald Reagan

For nearly a decade, Augusto Álvarez ran a financial services company in Mexico. He and his partner had hired a highly experienced person, Héctor Ochoa,[1] who they hoped would accelerate the organization's expansion across Mexico. Relieved to have completed their multi-month search, the partners transferred all of the relevant responsibilities to Ochoa starting on his first day. "The last thing we wanted to do was micromanage Héctor," Álvarez thought at the time. "He was the expert."

The problem was that Ochoa was given all of the operating responsibilities from day one, but almost no awareness of the culture of the company, the informal norms, and the business operations. By being strictly hands off, Álvarez had set Ochoa up to fail. Despite Ochoa's impeccable credentials, within six months Álvarez asked Ochoa to resign.

Vigilant, clear, and supportive onboarding is as important to successful hiring as interviews or reference checks. The *Harvard Business Review* reports that 40–60% of new hires fail within 18 months.[2] Much of this has to do with poor onboarding. Today we know that employees who go through a structured onboarding process are nearly two-thirds more likely to be with the company after three years than those who don't.[3] Given the effort required to hire someone, a proper onboarding process is one of the highest returns you'll get on your invested time.

The 100-Day Window

Whether the job entails assembling tacos, welding pipe, or managing a team of software developers, for any new hire the first 100 days of a new job are chockfull of uncertainty and awkwardness. Every organization has different standards, norms, and expectations, and it takes time for new team members to absorb and learn these.

But after 100 days, most of this uncertainty goes away. An inertia sets in as new employees develop a routine and familiarity.[4] They know who to call when their laptop crashes, the best place to park their car, and which grocery store is on the way home. They've figured out how the new health plan works.

The 100-day window is also when friendships develop. Most people arrive at work knowing no one, and that's unsettling, especially considering that many of our primary social needs are fulfilled at work. Research at the Yale School of Management shows that team members who have strong work friendships are healthier, happier, and significantly more engaged with their work.[5] This is increasingly more important as Gen Z'ers and millennials report the highest rate of work friendships compared to their older coworkers,[6] yet post-pandemic remote work patterns put these connections at risk.

All of this matters because a comfortable routine, friendships, and workplace familiarity are ranked as primary reasons people remain in their job. The *Wall Street Journal* reports that companies that are aligned with a strong onboarding process throughout the 100-day window reported drops in turnover of more than 35%.[7]

Strategies for the 100-Day Window

Of course, like Álvarez, you're anxious for your new hire to work their magic. Meanwhile, new hires are generally eager to show off their skills, and because they may worry that they're supposed to know all the answers on day one, they're reluctant to ask for help—especially if it relates to making friends, learning workplace norms, or being trained in their own areas of expertise. But take your time. Your organization survived for many weeks, or maybe even months, without this new hire—and you have one shot at getting the transition right.

An awareness of the criticality of the 100-day window has taken off throughout corporate America. Carrier Corporation, with 58,000 employees, addressed the issue by creating a three-month "buddy" program, pairing each new hire with a seasoned team member. CVS Health is so focused on the 100-day window that it offers a bonus to get new hires to stay for three months. To CVS Health's way of thinking, if it can get new hires over the anxiety of the first 100 days, it has a much higher shot at keeping them long term. Marissa Andrada, chief people officer at Chipotle, said to the *Wall Street Journal*, "If you see someone hit the three-month mark, the reality is they're going to be here for at least a year."[8] Which is why, after implementing a new shift schedule, better explanations of benefits, and improving its up-front training of operating procedures, Chipotle achieved a material reduction in turnover.

Begin by welcoming the new hire to your organization in a consequential way. Make it an event, not a to-do item to cross off your list. My friend Amy Errett, the chief executive officer of Madison Reed, told me how she introduces new team members at the company-wide Wednesday lunch. Her hair care company's revenues have tripled in the last three years, which makes retaining good hires essential to its future growth. With such a large company, the lunch happens remotely, and new hires have balloons as their background so everyone knows who has joined that week. The hiring manager offers an engaging and personal introduction (not a dry recitation of the person's resume), and then asks the new hire to reveal "two truths and a lie" about themselves. The entire company votes on which is the lie, and afterward the new employee announces which was the lie. In so doing, within the first week every employee knows the person's name and something about him or her. When they see them in the lunchroom, they know not let the new team member eat alone.

Rather than trusting each manager to get it right, Amy sets a culture of "this is how we welcome people," institutionalizes her process, and creates systems at Madison Reed that allow the company to introduce hundreds of people every year with fanfare.

But the welcome is only the beginning. You'll need to set up a schedule of lunches, and possibly dinners, with other team members. If applicable, include outside constituents such as customers and suppliers. Because these relationships are formed over the entire 100-day window, don't cram them all into the first week, but instead over a three- to four-week period.

When you hire new managers, avoid the mistake of giving them direct reports immediately, as Álvarez did with Ochoa. Allow them about a week to roam the organization before assuming any operating responsibility, so they can get to know people in other departments and meet with customers and vendors outside their functional area. For instance, your new controller might use this time to visit customers, observe operations in the warehouse, and watch your product being manufactured. As you transition operating responsibility, do so gradually and serially, adding direct reports one at a time, preferably separated by one or two weeks.

In parallel, make any training program required, not optional. Signal that training and orientation is a priority not to be canceled or postponed. Include in such training an indoctrination into the culture, values, and norms of the company—all of which is an elaborate way of saying: *This is how we act, and how we get things done.* As you explain the culture, values, and norms, avoid platitudes or generalities such as, "We have a culture of full transparency" or "We put the customer first!" What new hires instead want to know is the nitty-gritty stuff like whether people socialize after work, how are meetings run, and what the boss is *really* like. Don't make them guess or force them to read between the lines; just tell them.

Clarity with Support

As you begin to give your new hire operating responsibility, meet regularly one-on-one during the first three weeks. In these meetings, check to make sure the scheduled onboarding activity is happening and that training sessions and lunches are not being cancelled.

When it is time to transfer tasks to the new hire, communicate your expectations by creating a list of the outcomes using the *subskills* discussed in Chapter 12 (Delegating). For example, let's assume we've hired Rachel as the new finance supervisor. We might initially develop a list of outcomes for the first quarter:

- Replace the accounts payable manager.
- Propose a new health insurance plan.
- Lower past due receivables by half.
- Close the financials by the 10th of the month.
- Negotiate a leasing contract for new vehicle purchases.
- Put in place a company-wide procurement policy.
- Automate the employee expense reimbursement process.

This list is too long. Rachel is being set up for failure. Your job is to rein in your own expectations. Begin with only those items that involve learning the basics of the job or that address time-sensitive issues. Take, for example, replacing the accounts payable manager. As we know from the previous chapter, proper hiring is time-consuming, and anyway you'll need to indoctrinate Rachel with your hiring process before she begins reviewing candidates. That can wait. Next, who cares if the outdated expense reimbursement process remains in place another month or so? That too can wait. On the other hand, your health plan is up for renewal so a decision must be made, and if Rachel waits too long she'll never be able to collect those past due receivables.

- ~~Replace the accounts payable manager.~~
- Propose a new health insurance plan.
- Lower past due receivables by half.
- Close the financials by the 10th of the month.
- ~~Negotiate a leasing contract for new vehicle purchases.~~
- ~~Put in place a company-wide procurement policy.~~
- ~~Automate the employee expense reimbursement process.~~

These trade-offs are less difficult than you think because it is always *easier to add than subtract*. You can later add more things to her plate if you were overly conservative, but it is hard to take away tasks once they are delegated to her and she's begun working on them. There is virtually no penalty to missing low, but the consequences of an overly aggressive list can mean overwhelming, and then losing, a great hire.

Build a Vigilance Process

No matter how well you apply the subskill of good hiring, the process is imperfect. You will make hiring mistakes. Having observed them in the work environment versus the artificial setting of an interview, you'll know more about a new hire in the first couple of weeks than in the entire hiring process combined.

The *vigilance process* is critical because your best chance at saving a good hire who gets off to a difficult start is to address the concerns inside the 100-day window. The headwind you face is a formidable *confirmation bias* that impacts your likelihood of making good decisions. No one wants to admit they made a hiring mistake, especially if it means letting someone go and then restarting the hiring process. Which is why a mental commitment to be objective won't cut it. The antidote is to put in place a deliberate vigilance process.

As a first step, soon after they accept the offer, write down the key assumptions you made in your hiring decision. What qualities did this person have that made you enthusiastic about them? What did you identify as shortcomings or concerns? These should be short declarative sentences, with some reference to the supporting evidence and your hiring scorecard. During the 100-day window, actively look for any data to confirm or reject these key assumptions. For example, if the interview process raised concerns about whether the new hire may treat subordinates coarsely, test that concern by discreetly checking in with her or his staff, paying attention to nonverbal cues as they talk about their new boss.

Then, with the original hiring team (excluding any of the new hire's direct subordinates), set specific checkpoints at the 30-day mark and at the close of the 100-day window. These checkpoints are the heart and lungs of the vigilance process. Informal conversations are not a substitute for a process. At each of these two checkpoints, read aloud the hiring scorecard and the key assumptions you wrote down at the time of hiring. Every person present needs to arrive prepared to comment, as you ask each if they believe the candidate has met or exceeded those assumptions, and then to what extent and in what way. Next, ask what they would change about this person if they could. No one is perfect. Don't let anyone off the hook without responding. Lastly, poll the team to see whether, if the employee were to resign, they would be relieved, neutral, or devastated.

You may be tempted to race through these questions. Don't. Odds are good that if you *hired for outcomes*, you brought in a winner. But no one hires at a 100% success rate, and while it's forgivable to make a bad hire, it's poor leadership to take months to identify and admit a mistake.

During those occasions when you realize you made a hiring mistake, you may be reluctant to act quickly, wanting to give them every chance to succeed. Know that you do them no favors by delaying the inevitable. They deserve to be at a company, and in a position, where they can shine. As well, by quickly accepting the mistake, you make their subsequent job search easier: they may characterize those first weeks as probationary, and not even include your company on their resume. Selfishly, by being decisive you may also be able to jump-start your hiring process by contacting your second- or third-choice candidates who may still be available.

A Final Thought . . .

The most common mistake I see when managers implement the *subskill* of onboarding is to rely on the new team member to manage the pace and fidelity of the process themselves. Less skillful managers ignore the 100-day window and put the burden on new hires to admit if they're feeling overwhelmed or ask to slow things down. But this seldom works. It's unrealistic to expect a new person to report when training sessions, led by their colleagues or supervisor, are cancelled. Same with those carefully scheduled lunches. They will be slow to raise their hand in surrender if you've given them too much too soon, or to raise concerns about the process.

To take full advantage of the power of the 100-day window, hiring managers must make it their responsibility to observe and enforce the plan. While this takes additional time, the payback is enormous in terms of a smooth transition, a faster identification of a mistake, and lower turnover.

The 100-Day Window

1. Make the welcome process an event, not something to cross off your to-do list.

2. Institutionalize the process so that it is done consistently throughout the organization.

3. Set up a social/meal schedule with those people critical to the new hire's success.

4. Explain the company's policies and procedures, benefits, and other administrative practices.

5. Explain the key elements of the organization's culture, values, and norms.

6. For managers, gradually transition their direct reports and departmental responsibilities.

7. Create time for the new hire to wander and observe other departments and to meet people.

8. *It's easier to add than subtract.* Be conservative with what you put on their plate.

9. Directly check in with the new hire to make sure that the training programs are not cancelled or postponed.

10. Vigilance. Set specific checkpoints midway and at the close of the 100-day window to make sure you made the correct hiring decision:
    a. Reconvene the original hiring team (excepting any direct reports).
    b. Read aloud the hiring scorecard, and the key hiring assumptions.
    c. Ask three questions:
        i. Has the candidate met or exceeded the hiring assumptions?
        ii. What would you change about this person if you could?
        iii. If the employee were to resign, would you be relieved, neutral, or devastated?

3 Instant Performance Feedback

I absolutely believe that people, unless coached, never reach their maximum potential.

—Bob Nardelli, former CEO of Home Depot and Chrysler

When Steve Ballmer was CEO of Microsoft, he ran an employee evaluation program called "stack ranking." Every year, each business unit scored its employees against one another, rating them top to bottom. Stack ranking is thought to be one of the most destructive processes to happen at Microsoft.[1] As one developer noted, "If you were on a team of 10 people, you walked in the first day knowing that no matter how good everyone was, two people were going to get a great review, seven were going to get mediocre reviews, and one was going to get a terrible review." A similar system at General Electric was called "rank and yank" because those graded in the bottom 10% would be expected to resign or face dismissal.

Microsoft and GE were working off a 2,000-year-old feedback technique that, according to the *Harvard Business Review*, "drives neither employee engagement nor high performance."[2] These overly systematic approaches allow company leaders to imagine they have fulfilled their coaching responsibilities, while providing little in the way of useful feedback. Their employees feel the same way. A measly 14% of surveyed employees strongly agreed that their performance reviews helped them improve.

Classic performance reviews don't work because we're bad at rating one another along rigid dimensions. We can hardly capture the sum of a person's work in a single number or a label such as "meets expectations." The practice of conducting evaluations only once or twice a year is also subject to a *recency bias*, whereby we assign a higher probability of something happening again if it occurred recently. If Caroline and Jason performed at a similar level of competence throughout the year, but Jason's strongest work came just prior to the review period, while Caroline had multiple victories earlier in the year, in most cases Jason will be perceived as a better performer even though Caroline is the superstar—and in the case of Microsoft's or GE's former systems, this can result in serious consequences.

Fortunately, this archaic practice of periodic reviews once or twice a year is rapidly changing. Organizations like the consulting firm Accenture, which has more than 700,000 employees as of this writing, moved to instant performance feedback, or IPF. Pierre Nanterme, who was Accenture's CEO from 2011 until his death in 2019, explained: "We're done with the famous annual performance review, where once a year I'm going to share with you what I think about you." He went on to point out, "People want to know on an ongoing basis, 'Am I doing right? Am I moving in the right direction? Do you think I'm progressing?'"[3] Employees agree. They are more than five times as likely to prefer an IPF over an annual or semi-annual process.[4] For instance, when Adobe scrapped its annual review process for its 20,000-plus employees, hundreds of Adobe employees posted their support for trashing the old system in return for IPF.

Instant Performance Feedback over Annual Reviews

Paul English, whom I introduced in Chapter 1 (Hire for Outcomes), told me a story about working for Intuit after he sold his company to it. Intuit creates blockbuster products including TurboTax and QuickBooks, and Paul had become its vice president of technology. This was before founding

Kayak, and like many early leaders, Paul struggled with giving negative or blunt feedback. That was, until he experienced the value of IPF firsthand:

> *I was in a meeting with [Oracle CEO] Larry Ellison, who was interested in buying one of Intuit's businesses. The meeting did not go as hoped, and afterward, as we walked across Oracle's parking lot my boss said, "Paul, do you have a minute? I want to give you some feedback." He explained to me there in the parking lot that I had been ineffective responding to one of Ellison's questions, and then described why.*

In that moment, Paul saw how the best managers are always on the lookout for coachable moments. If his boss had waited even a few days to speak with him, Paul would have been unlikely to remember enough of the meeting's details to benefit from the comments; so too his boss would have forgotten particulars that would have helped Paul. What Paul and other effective managers have learned is that feedback is most effectual—positive and negative—when it is delivered as close to the time of the underlying event as possible. Don't save your thoughts for a bureaucratic semi-annual event. If it's feedback worth giving, it's worth delivering right away.

Radical Candor

Andy Dunn cofounded the apparel company Bonobos, which was eventually sold to Walmart for more than $300 million. Andy had been a guest in my class, when at dinner, we were talking about how to provide effective feedback. Andy took out his phone and said, "I want to show you something." It was an illustration developed by Kim Scott, the author of *Radical Candor: How to Get What You Want By Saying What You Mean* (Figure 3.1).[5]

Across the horizontal axis, Scott's framework measures a person's willingness to challenge directly. The vertical axis shows their capacity to care personally. What Scott observed is that most people either resist providing ongoing high-quality coaching out of a misperception that kindness requires being indirect, or they let bad news go unaddressed—which Scott terms Ruinous Empathy. Ruinous Empathy leads us to water down our feedback to near meaninglessness, leaving us personally unscathed and feeling better about ourselves, while failing our team.

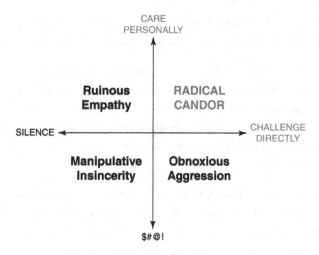

Figure 3.1 Radical Candor

Scott incorporates two principles to delivering quality feedback: caring personally and challenging directly. When done right, it's highly effective. Radical Candor runs counter to our instincts of not wanting to hurt others and in wanting to be liked. But being indirect about feedback is never kind—and being liked is a poor goal for a leader. As Scott writes, "Ruinous Empathy is seeing somebody with their fly down, but not wanting to embarrass them, saying nothing, with the result that 15 more people see them with their fly down."[6]

Meanwhile, Ruinous Empathy reduces the person's chance to improve, and since we are good at detecting insincerity, Ruinous Empathy leaves people uncertain as to where they really stand. Andy and I agreed that early in our careers we had both been guilty of a common form of Ruinous Empathy: the "feedback sandwich."[7] In a feedback sandwich, we first deliver a gratuitous compliment only to earn permission to say what we really want to say. We then offer the important feedback, then complete the sandwich by tossing in some reassuring words that only serve to reduce the impact of our feedback. In the example involving Paul English, a feedback sandwich might taste like this:

Paul, that was a great meeting with Oracle, and I like your style. Try, though, to always be as frank as you can with your answers, which you mostly do. And I'm glad to have you on the team!

The best way to implement Radical Candor across your organization is to spend several months soliciting it for yourself; in other words, invite your team to give you feedback. As Scott writes, "Prove you can take it before you start dishing it out." Make those moments frequent and uneventful. When you inevitably hear someone offer Ruinous Empathy, or serve you a feedback sandwich, ask that they rephrase the feedback with Radical Candor, or model it for them.

After this becomes ingrained in the culture, move next to offering only positive Radical Candor to the people who work for you. When you do so, call it out by name so they recognize what you're doing:

> *Hiro, I want to offer some Radical Candor. That report you just presented was exactly what we were looking for. What I liked specifically was how you were frank with the challenges facing our sales department, notably when you said . . .*

Once you have proven you can take Radical Candor yourself, modeled how best to receive critical feedback, and then offered Radical Candor in the form of positive feedback, shift to giving out a mix of positive and critical Radical Candor, always calling it out by name so they recognize what is happening:

> *Anya, I'd like to offer you some feedback in the form of Radical Candor. You're consistently arriving late for meetings, and the reason this is an issue is . . .*

For the first three months, aim for twice as many instances of positive feedback over negative feedback, but never confusing that with serving up a feedback sandwich. By implementing IPF and Radical Candor in this way, you'll ensure a smooth transition to meaningful feedback.

A Six-Part Framework for IPF

When I first became a CEO, my controller delivered the monthly financials more than 60 days after the end of the month. When I got the reports, I would either say nothing or disguise my concern in a feedback sandwich. In each subsequent month she'd fail to meet my expectation, and I'd serve her another sandwich. Things never improved, and eventually I let her go. In so doing I did both her and the company a disservice. As I matured as a manager,

I came to develop a six-part framework that created guardrails to ensure that I regularly provide effective IPF (Figure 3.2):

Expectation → Measurement → Feedback →
Obstacles → Support → Alignment

Figure 3.2 Framework for Feedback

If I had used this framework with my controller, instead of offering Ruinous Empathy, which may have cost her her job, I might have said:

> *I need the financials to be delivered to the team on a timely basis so we can use that information to make operational decisions (**expectation**). Absent an unusual circumstance, this needs to happen before the 15th of the following month (**measurement**). In the last two months we closed 55 days and 47 days after the end of the month (**feedback**). What problems are you facing getting the financials delivered before the 15th? (**obstacles**).*

Imagine she then described a delay in receiving information from the vice president of sales (**obstacle**). With this information, I might have said:

> *I'll speak with Ray about making sure we get you the sales commission information by the 5th of each month. That will be my responsibility (**support**).*

She might have also suggested the need to wait until she'd received all vendor invoices before closing the books. In this case I could have said:

> *As far as the vendor invoices, if any straggle in after the 10th of the month, I'm fine if you put them into the following month's financials (**support**).*

Unearthing legitimate obstacles, and then finding solutions, sets the table for the last step: alignment. There is an important difference between *agreement* and *alignment*. Effective leaders should listen carefully, but they do not require consensus in their choices. Decisions must be made, which at times members of your team will not agree with. For example, if my controller took the position that it was better to wait to issue the financials until after she'd received all vendor invoices, I might tell her:

> *I understand your position and understand your view. But I've decided we're going to take a different path. Now I need to know that this plan is something you can agree to (**alignment**).*

As you provide feedback, look for ways to frame it in their best interests. For example, by making this behavior change they will be more promotable, they will sell more products and earn higher commissions, or their employee turnover will drop, which will improve their area's performance. The more they feel the change benefits them, the more likely they will make the transformation.

A Final Thought . . .

Before running for president and later becoming a US senator, Mitt Romney led the private equity firm Bain Capital through some of its best years, generating returns for investors that exceeded 100% annually.[8] I was fortunate to have him as an investor and board member of a company I ran, and I recall a conversation where he described a fundamental tenet of Bain's strategy: spend time on investments that show the most promise and limit your time with those with low prospects. Mitt told me about one investment in particular: "Our range of outcomes was losing all of our money, or maybe get our investment back. But we have investments where the outcomes might range from a 3X return to a 10X return, which is where we spend our time and focus."

The same is true with your team. Most leaders neglect their star performers, or those with the potential to become stars, and dwell on those who have the least potential. They view coaching as a process of fixing problems instead of maximizing performance. Not only will IPF raise up your superstars, but you'll increase the chances they stay on your team. Employees who report that they're not adequately recognized at work are three times more likely to say they'll quit in the next year.[9]

You'll get far more leverage spending time providing IPF to your stars than everyone else combined. Focus on your stars, using IPF to turn good team members into great ones, and reducing the risk that you will lose your very best performers by not providing them with the coaching they want.

Instant Performance Feedback

1. Replace periodic reviews with instant performance feedback (IPF).

2. Avoid numeric ratings and labels.

3. Discuss the specific behavior you want to reinforce or avoid, not provide generalized comments about the person.

4. Be on the lookout for "coachable moments" and deliver IPF (positive and negative) as soon as practical.

5. Use a six-part framework for IPF to create a structure to your comments.

   Expectation → Measurement → Feedback →
   Obstacles → Support → Alignment

6. Scott's Radical Candor is caring personally and challenging directly. To implement Radical Candor, take the following five steps:
   a. First, spend several months soliciting it for yourself.
   b. Second, offer only positive Radical Candor to your direct reports.
   c. Third, give out a mix of positive and critical Radical Candor.
   d. Fourth, fully implement Radical Candor with your direct reports.
   e. Fifth, repeat these steps with each subsequent layer of your organization.

7. Don't serve up a feedback sandwich to ease the process for yourself.

8. Frame feedback on why it matters to them and why accepting the feedback is in their best interests.

9. Focus mostly on your stars. Spend most of your time turning good team members into great ones.

4 The 360 Review

Criticism may not be agreeable, but it is necessary. It fulfills the same function as pain in the human body; it calls attention to an unhealthy state of things.

—Sir Winston Churchill

The idea of getting feedback from a person's peers and subordinates was first instituted by the US military in World War I.[1] The goal was to get a sense of a soldier's readiness for promotion. Over time, more and more organizations adopted the technique, which today is known as a "360 Review" or "360," so called because the idea is to solicit feedback from everyone who interacts with the subject—above, below, and beside them in the organization chart.

Two experts writing in the *Harvard Business Review* likened the 360 technique to a GPS system: just as getting an accurate location requires multiple satellites, feedback from your manager, peers, and direct reports pinpoints the way to understanding your own effectiveness.[2] Properly implemented, a 360 is immensely valuable. Companies that effectively use 360s are better able to recruit and retain top performers and develop talent, leading to a more effective and competitive organization.

While the observations of peers and subordinates are powerful management tools, the process can be intimidating, and the results of poor implementation can be devastating. At Stanford, I teach a case in which three coworkers submitted comments about a manager whom we'll call Tony.[3]

As part of the organization's process, these anonymously submitted comments were shared verbatim with Tony:

> *Tony is difficult to work with. Sometimes he's happy, and then he'll be angry. Bottom line, Tony is not fun to work with.*
>
> *Tony takes the glory for himself. There are several of us on the marketing team, but I always hear him talking about all the work he's done. What about the rest of us?*
>
> *He never gives us feedback. He asks for what he needs and that's it. I have no idea if my work is any good.*

After reading the comments, Tony felt insecure as he wondered who had said what. He assumed that he had lost the confidence of his team. Understandably embarrassed and hurt, Tony resigned. Instead of the process lifting him to a higher level of performance, it became a forum for anonymous complaints and led to him feeling unwelcome and unliked. Tony had areas for development, but those issues were coachable, and he could have been a successful long-term member of the team. But the damage was nonetheless lasting.

360 reviews are a powerful strategic weapon in today's competitive marketplace. Fortunately, there are a few straightforward steps to implementing the subskill of 360 reviews and avoiding what happened to Tony.

Start Slow to Go Fast

A properly implemented 360 process can take as long as two years. In the first phase, conduct just one 360 review—on yourself. Explain to your team the rationale of the program, the logistics of how to submit feedback, the rules of confidentiality, and how the information will be used. The process can be as straightforward as using email, using one of the many app or software programs available, or being managed by an outside provider.

Begin the 360 on just yourself. Explain that confidentiality allows people to express genuine and complete feelings and eliminates the temptation to provide positive feedback to gain favor. No matter how clear you are, don't expect your employees to straightaway accept pledges of confidentiality or that it's safe to send candid feedback upward. You'll need to demonstrate the integrity of the process by being diligent about making sure breeches in confidentiality don't happen. Remind them that the responses should express Radical Candor and that anonymity is not an opportunity to practice Obnoxious Aggression.

Then make the results of your 360 known company-wide, actively modeling how to respond to both positive and negative feedback. As you do so, be prepared for some painful revelations. The first time I received feedback from my team, I was told that I came off like a person with ice water running through their veins. This was over 30 years ago, and I still remember how embarrassed I felt. Nonetheless, the mission is less about you receiving useful feedback (although you will) and more about modeling the 360 process— which means you have to be especially careful to model how to receive their feedback, even if it means you discover that you have a reputation for having ice water in your veins.

A few months later, conduct a second round with your direct reports. Repeat the process with these same people until the practice is working just as you designed. Only after you have both yourself and your direct reports receiving and responding well to 360 data should you extend it to the next organizational layer of the company. Then, as you roll it out, pay close attention to how your managers implement it in their departments so not to undermine the foundation you carefully poured and set.

A layer-by-layer process is slower than a full roll-out, and you might be tempted to accelerate the process. But a rushed 360 implementation that leads to mistakes severely damages morale and trust (as we saw in the case with Tony), and may make it impossible to later implement the program at all.

Collecting the Information

If you Google "best 360 questions to ask," you'll get more than 500 million results, mostly listing generalized questions that include forced rankings of 1 to 5 or gradations that span "strongly disagree" to "strongly agree." But a 360 review is like instant performance feedback (IPF), where rankings and generalized comparisons are seldom actionable. Two people might give a different rank to the same person because they differ in the meaning of the phrase *demonstrates strong leadership*, or they have separate assumptions of what it means to be a 4.0 versus a 5.0 in "strong leadership."

Instead of rankings and numbers, focus on the priorities of your particular organization. For instance, let's consider an organization that prioritizes speedy delivery. An effective 360 question might be:

> *To what extent does the individual contribute to the goal of speedy delivery in their day-to-day work? Please provide specific examples to illustrate your conclusion.*

Note that the question could have begun with, "Does the person contribute to the goal of . . ." but that allows for a "yes" or a "no" response, which will provide far less actionable and detailed information. The phrasing "To what extent does the person contribute to the goal . . ." forces the respondent to provide a nuanced reply, which will better reflect the person's unique contribution, and provides better data to impact the person's future performance.

As you write the questions, be sure to keep them simple, avoiding the latest business jargon (e.g., "full transparency," "core competency," "pivot"), which may not be universally understood. Limit the number of questions to fewer than seven. With lengthy questionnaires, respondents put less time into each question, leaving you with hastily responded to answers. You'll get the best results by sticking to a few probing and open-ended questions that can be answered in 15 to 20 minutes.

The Three Cs

The 360 process is not a forum where people get to post whatever they want, in whatever way they want. The responses are intended to provide feedback that can lead to behavior change, but not an excuse for venting or unactionable complaints. Nonetheless, despite this aspiration some of your team members will do just that. Which is why for a 360 review process to function properly, you need to apply the *three Cs*:

- Curate the feedback.
- Create a personal growth plan.
- Close the loop.

Curate the Feedback

Begin by eliminating negative comments that won't lead to material behavior change. "Tony is incredibly difficult to work with" may be true, but it's not actionable. On the other hand, "He never gives us feedback" can be addressed by Tony. Curating the feedback removes trivial gripes that will occupy emotional space and interfere with important developmental issues. Follow a simple rule: if it's not actionable, let it go.

Summarize the general themes rather than provide raw comments. Poorly phrased feedback can be, and should be, reworded by you or another manager. This also allows for a higher degree of confidentiality as direct comments are easier to trace to their source and often lead to speculation as to who said what. Next, generate a summary of a few prioritized and actionable themes. For example, in the case of Tony, consider these comments, which are related to one another and should be summarized into a single theme:

> *Tony takes the glory for himself. There are several of us on the marketing team, but I always hear him talking about all the work he's done. What about the rest of us?*
>
> *He never gives us feedback. He asks for what he needs and that's it. I have no idea if my work is any good.*

As you curate, you do not have to accept every comment at face value. You may choose to follow up with the respondent and verify that any one observation is shared by others. For instance, I was once asked by a CEO to conduct a 360 review with his direct reports. One vice president said, "He just doesn't care." The underlying feedback struck me as unactionable, so I followed up with him and learned his concern was that the CEO had committed to quarterly company meetings, but they were taking place only two to three times a year.

I verified the concern, learning that others were also disappointed and felt de-prioritized by the cancelled meetings. Instead of an unactionable and emotional comment ("He just doesn't care"), I created actionable, verified, and useful 360 feedback.

Create a Personal Growth Plan

When I passed along the feedback regarding how the CEO had skipped quarterly meetings, he agreed with the observations and told me that he would do better. But "do better" is not a plan, and I doubt he was missing those meetings on purpose—the obstacles he faced still existed. Instead, I employed elements of the IPF framework (Figure 4.1):

Expectation → Measurement → Feedback
→ Obstacles → Support → Alignment

Figure 4.1 Framework for a Growth Plan

The *expectation, measurement,* and *feedback* were already captured in the 360 review, so I spent the time understanding why he failed to hold the meetings (*obstacles*). He said that he'd forget, he'd get busy, or that other projects would intervene, making it hard to find a time on the calendar. We agreed that those obstacles were not going away on their own, which is why his original approach of "do better" was not likely to succeed.

With this in mind, we co-created a plan to schedule the first Thursday of every quarter for company meetings. That solved the scheduling issue. Then we assigned his assistant to take responsibility for logistics, communication, and refreshments. Lastly, I told him that I'd mark my own calendar, and I would shoot him an email after the first two meetings to ask how it went (*support*). He agreed with the plan (*alignment*). Unsurprisingly, because we created a personal growth plan, he never again missed a quarterly meeting. As a special dividend, his team gained confidence in the 360 process, which created a virtuous cycle as he expanded the 360 program throughout the company.

Close the Loop

A study involving 4,000 employees found that "when employees don't feel heard or feel their needs aren't met, they are less likely to maximize their talents and experience at their workplace—and are more likely to seek those opportunities elsewhere."[4] People want to be heard and yet are generally rational about the expected level of change. Not everything peers and subordinates want is good for the organization, and 360 reviews are not an opportunity to make demands, create development plans for others, or establish the organization's priorities.

Which is why it is essential that after asking for feedback, you close the loop with those who provided the responses, and that you let them know what—if anything—you plan to do even if the answer is you plan to change nothing.

In closing the loop, follow this four-part framework that I learned from Jim Ellis, a faculty member at Stanford and highly successful entrepreneur:

First: "This is the feedback I received . . ."

Second: "Here are some things that cannot change, and let me explain why . . ."

Third: "These are issues I agree with, but won't be able to work on them until . . ."

Fourth: "These are the things I plan to work on immediately . . ."

As you close the loop, make sure to create a culture of self-improvement, not of apology. It is critical that you model your reactions to the 360 responses not as confessions, defenses, or apologies such as, "I'm really sorry I've acted that way." A 360 review is not a reward and punishment exercise. It's where everyone participates in a process of iterative self-improvement. If you want to maximize results, the culture should be about elevating one another, not identifying wrongdoing. This is not to say a leader should never apologize, just that doing so within a 360 process can degrade the primary purpose of the program.

However, if you receive feedback like "ice water runs through your veins," while you should avoid an apology, you can use that as an opportunity to show your human side, reinforce your willingness to improve, and help brand the 360 process as a program for elevating one another. For example:

> *That was not fun to read, and I must admit it hit me hard. But the more I reflected on how I react at times—and having talked with some of my personal advisors, as well as my wife—I came to realize this is indeed an area I need to work on. I'm thankful to those of you who brought this to my attention. Here's how I plan to work on . . .*

None of this will happen naturally. Be hands on, as the integrity of the 360 process affects the entire organization, and until it's ingrained into the DNA of your team members, you must be hands-on in ensuring that the three Cs are done always and precisely, including reviewing the curation by your managers, creating personal growth plans, and witnessing early examples of closing the loop.

A Final Thought . . .

In my earliest days as a manager, I didn't employ 360 reviews. I told myself that I knew what I needed to know and that we were a small enough organization where we could all speak openly to one another. I imagined a 360 akin to a group-therapy session and not a process to acquire critical data that would increase my competitiveness. In reflecting now, I also suspect I was intimidated by what people might write. If you feel any of these emotions, instead of doing what I did, give it a try. In avoiding 360s, I missed out on a powerful tool in building an enduring team.

The 360 Review

1. Start slow to go fast. Implementation may take as long as two years.

2. Do not use numeric ratings and labels.

3. Focus on your company's specific priorities. Structure the questions so that they cannot be answered with a "yes" or "no."

4. Limit the number of questions to a few probing and open-ended questions that can be answered in 15 to 20 minutes.

5. Implement through these steps and in this order:
   a. First, conduct a 360 review on just yourself.
   b. Second, make the results known company-wide and model how to respond to feedback.
   c. Third, conduct a 360 review with your direct reports.
   d. Fourth, based on success, expand the 360 review across each subsequent layer of your organization.

6. After receiving the responses follow the three Cs:
   a. *Curate* the feedback, removing any obnoxious aggression and summarizing general themes.
   b. *Create* a personal growth plan that addresses *obstacles, support,* and *alignment.*
   c. *Close* the loop by addressing four areas.

"This is the feedback I received . . ."

"Here are some things that cannot change, and let me explain why . . ."

"These are issues I agree with, but won't be able to work on them until . . ."

"These are the things I plan to work on immediately . . ."

---

7. Create a culture of self-improvement, not apology.

Ten Examples of 360 Review Questions

1. How does [name] positively contribute to our company culture of [specific cultural attribute]?

2. What areas could [name] improve upon in his/her contribution to our culture of [specific cultural attribute]?

3. How has [name] contributed to the goal of [specific company goal]?

4. If you were [name's] supervisor, and were to offer one developmental goal for next year for [name], what would that be?

5. How has [name] helped you achieve your professional goals?

6. If a friend asked you how to describe [name] in his/her professional role, what would you tell her/him?

7. Does [name] make you more or less likely to stay with [company], and why?

8. How well does [name] set and adhere to the company priorities?

9. If a friend were to go work for/with [name], what advice would you give your friend to maximize his/her success with [name]?

10. If this person were to be transferred to another position in our company, why might you want to follow her/him, and what would be the reasons you might instead decide to remain where you are?

5 Coaching Underperformance

Words are sacred. They deserve respect. If you get the right ones, in the right order, you can nudge the world a little.

—Tom Stoppard

I once had a member of my team who was struggling with his harsh treatment of people, one that was inconsistent with our culture. I could have written him off as a poor cultural fit and let him go, but I knew if I could fix the issues, it would be better for the company. He was a strong performer otherwise, and the position would be hard to fill in a competitive hiring marketplace. But I needed a framework for determining whether his issues were coachable, and if so, how to maximize the chances of success.

Despite the clear evidence that many underperformers can be coached to success, few managers and companies know how to do so. An incredible 40% of companies reported that they would *not* rehire most or all of their coworkers, and yet at the same time they are unwilling to address the areas of underperformance![1]

In the case of the manager I just described, using the processes outlined in this chapter I accepted that the issues he struggled with were serious and not going away on their own, but also that he was coachable. This chapter is not about those occasional mistakes or course corrections that you address with *instant performance feedback (IPF)*. This chapter is about how best to coach those team members who are underperforming in a way that is unsustainable and, if not addressed, calls to question whether they belong with the organization.

Four-Step Process

Coaching underperformance is seldom urgent, and for that reason we postpone the unpleasant confrontation, which generally makes the situation more extreme and harder to address. We make up stories about how the situation will correct itself if we just give it time. But that seldom happens in real life. To protect against this, twice a year evaluate your team using these four sure-fire steps.

First, note on your organization chart which team members you would rank as A, B, or C. Ranking people in this way may seem inconsistent with the case I made against forced ranking. The difference is there is no requirement to have a predetermined distribution of A, B, and C employees.

Don't rush this step. Be intentional about these categories, using an A rating to indicate the person has a 90% chance of achieving top 10% results. The B rating reflects those with the potential to become A or are in positions that do not require an A level employee.[2] C represents those who are frequently failing to meet expectations or struggling in areas that are material to their success.

There is a natural tendency to lower or raise the bar based on your personal connection with the person, so begin by first making this a left-brain exercise, using the part of your brain that is orderly and analytical and relying as much as possible on objective observations. Leveraging the skills you learned from Chapter 1 (Hire for Outcomes), search for evidence of successes or failures as they relate to specific *outcomes* or *attributes*.

Second, bring the right-brain into play, the intuitive part of your thought process. In this step, with team members that you marked as B or C, imagine them coming into your office and resigning for a great opportunity. You've now eliminated the uncomfortable step of having to fire them. With this, consider whether in your gut you would feel relieved, neutral, or devastated?

Third, beginning with the words "In three years . . . ," sketch out what you expect your organization chart to look like.[3] Include names and titles. See who will have a role in the future version of your organization. As you imagine your star team, can you picture this person with you then, or are they just filling a current need?

Fourth and last, ask yourself: "If I were filling a vacancy, knowing what I know today, would I hire this person for that position for 125% of their current salary?"

These four questions take about half an hour, twice a year. When done methodically, you'll identify the people you need to focus on retaining and developing, and those who have more fundamental concerns that need addressing.

Coachable or Not?

You'll next need to determine whether the person is coachable. I recall a conversation I once had with a former student who needed to replace her director of sales. She'd heard the expression, "Once you think about firing someone, it's already too late." I disagreed. When you consider the cost and risk of replacing a person, the more pragmatic solution is to try and coach them to success—provided they are coachable.

I posed a question to her: "What behaviors would need to change for this sales director to become an A?" She told me he would need to be "way better" at recruiting, hiring, and retaining salespeople. "Not good enough," I said, pressing her to describe the specific behavior changes she wanted to see in the person's hiring procedure. She couldn't answer the question, and I asked her to come back when she could.

Her eventual list included many of the steps associated with *hiring for outcomes*, such as his failure to conduct reference checks or implementing a formal onboarding process—none of which I learned she'd discussed with him in any of her prior feedback moments.

Behaviors generally fall into three categories: *knowledge-based, skill-based,* and *attribute-based.* A controller who is not current with applicable tax laws has a knowledge-based deficiency; weaknesses with financial modeling would be skill-based issue; an inability to work well with others is an attribute-based problem. These distinctions are critical to identify because knowledge and skills are generally coachable, while attributes such as intelligence, ambition, attitude, trust, and emotional IQ are difficult to coach.

If you find yourself with an employee who is suffering from an attribute-based issue, you face an uphill battle. Fortunately, there are five questions that almost always lead to the answer as to whether someone with an attribute-based concern is coachable:[4]

Is the person taking ownership of the problem?

Are they volunteering ideas for a solution?

Do you sense any contrition?

Are they willing to make compromises in their position to solve the problem?

Are their fundamental values compatible with those of the organization?

To form a point of view, speak with the person in a way that addresses these questions, and listen with deep curiosity. This is not the time to coach, convince, or to help that person change. You are gathering data to determine whether this person is coachable. For that you need to mostly listen.

Lastly, while ethical lapses are not the same as attribute-based deficiencies, a single misstep may not be grounds for giving up on a person. Be mindful of the phrase I learned from H. Irving Grousbeck: "The worst thing you ever did is a boundary marker, not a centerline." We have all said and done things we're not proud of. The question to ask is whether the person's actions were *indicative* of who he or she is and do they represent a pattern, or were they an *exception*? In the case of an exception, rather than judge and punish such people, help them return to the path they have set for themselves. You'll find it personally rewarding and a better demonstration of your own humanity.

Development Plan

Having identified an area of underperformance and determined the issues are coachable, employ the key concepts from IPF (Figure 5.1):

Expectation → Measurement → Feedback →
Obstacles → Support → Alignment

Figure 5.1 Framework for a Growth Plan

In these more severe situations, it is tempting to use statements that describe people generally rather than focus on the specific *behaviors* you want to change. In the example of my former student, instead of saying to the director of sales, "You need to be way better at recruiting, hiring, and retaining salespeople," which will almost certainly fail, pick one skill area—for example, onboarding—and spend time helping him master that *subskill*. You don't need to rebuild Rome in a day. If they succeed with the first challenge, and show a willingness to learn more, then move to the next desired behavior change.

Since the person's job is at stake, you need to memorialize the plan in writing. This is not to lay the groundwork for an eventual dismissal. If the culture in your company becomes one where your employees believe that getting a written plan is the company's way of papering the file in anticipation of a dismissal, hardly anyone will graduate to success. A development plan must be a genuine attempt at coaching to success. In my own case, two-thirds of the employees who received a written development plan succeeded and remained with the organization—often extending to promotions.

We often steer away from putting the plan in writing because doing so might appear severe—yet this is exactly why it's valuable. We owe it to someone whose job is at risk to make clear the consequences of failure: *If this does not change, you can't remain here.* The written process also forces a level of precision as you confront what needs to happen for success, and a written development plan reduces the risk of miscommunication.

I suggest using a standardized format for your development plans, applying Radical Candor, and incorporating the steps of IPF to carefully articulate areas such as *measurement* and *obstacles*. To make sure the whole organization follows your process, consider a policy that no employee may be dismissed without your approval, unless that employee was previously put on a development plan.

Set-Up-to-Fail Syndrome

The *set-up-to-fail syndrome*[5] describes a dysfunctional cycle common with coaching people who are underperforming in an aspect of their job that dooms them to failure. In the set-up-to-fail syndrome, a coachable issue is brought to the attention of the employee. But instead of applying the concepts from IPF and focusing on obstacles, support, and alignment, the manager's level of watchfulness rises, which signals a lack of confidence. The employee senses that doubt and becomes more tentative. As a result, the watchfulness increases and the employee retreats further, creating a ruinous cycle.

Avoid the set-up-to-fail syndrome by making three unambiguous points to employees being coached. First, that you *believe* they can succeed. Second, that you *want* them to succeed. Third, that once corrected the issue will not hang over them going forward, or as the monkey Rafiki says in the Disney film *The Lion King*, "It doesn't matter. It's in the past." By way of example:

> *If I didn't think you could succeed, we'd be discussing a transition. If you buy into this plan, you'll succeed. You're a valuable team member and losing you would be a disappointment to the organization, but even more so to me personally. I want you to succeed, and I will put in whatever it takes to ensure your success. And once this is behind us, it will be behind us.*

Lastly, as a final element to the set-up-to-fail syndrome, remember that a development plan is often embarrassing. That alone can impact their chances of success if it becomes known to others and becomes a source of anxiety for the affected person. To reduce this impact, keep the circle small and, if possible, make a commitment to confidentiality. In so doing, you create the greatest chance for them to succeed—not just with the development plan, but as an ongoing team member.

The "No Asshole" Rule

Early in my career, working at the consulting firm McKinsey & Company, I had a boss who held us to a high standard. Yet, he got what he wanted by berating people, at times leaving his team humiliated. On one occasion, after I'd worked three consecutive 15-hour days, he shamed me in front of others over a typo. My mistakes were real, but rather than using concepts of IPF, his strategy was to humiliate me into change.

My Stanford colleague Robert Sutton would say that despite my former boss's high standards, he wasn't worth the damage to the organization. Sutton developed the *No Asshole Rule*.[6] In his book, which is carefully researched, Sutton describes "The Dirty Dozen,"[7] those characteristics such as insults or shaming, and the people who leave others feeling oppressed, humiliated, or worse about themselves. To Sutton, these people are not worth the damage they inflict, no matter how effective they may be in their job. He points out that we often fail to consider the total cost of having an asshole in the organization, which includes hard-dollar costs such as the loss of great employees, time spent dealing with the fallout, and demotivation of talented team members.

Being an asshole is almost always an uncoachable attribute. If you find assholes in your organization, alert them to the issue, put them on a very short time frame, and if they do not respond to the steps outlined in this chapter, apply Sutton's rule.

A Final Thought . . .

In *Good to Great*, Jim Collins coins the phrase "on the bus," referring to those people you want with you on the organization's journey. He writes: "The executives who ignited the transformations from *good to great* did not first figure out where to drive the bus and then get people to take it there. No, they first got the right people on the bus (and the wrong people off the bus) and then figured out where to drive it."[8]

No doubt you will find situations where the individual has the attributes of a great team member but is in the wrong position—Collins calls this being in the wrong seat of the bus. I once had a situation where a vice president responsible for managing 900 employees wasn't succeeding. Yet, he was an excellent fit within the organization, experienced, and had all the right attributes. Rather than lose him, we asked him to create and lead a new department that better aligned with his skills. He was excellent in that position, reminding me of the saying: "Don't try to race sheep. Don't try to herd racehorses."[9] After we sold the company, I hired him again, and 20 years later we're still friends, have invested in businesses together, and sit together on boards of directors.

Coaching Underperformance

1. Twice a year ask yourself four questions about your team:

    How would I rank my team members: A, B, or C?

    If the person resigned, would I be relieved or devastated?

    "In three years . . ." what does my organization chart look like?

    "If I were filling a vacancy, knowing what I know today, would I hire this person for the same position at 125% her/his current salary?"

2. Focus on *behaviors,* not the person.

3. Identify what specific *behaviors* would need to change for the person to become an A-player.

4. Determine whether any deficiencies are knowledge-based, skill-based, or attribute-based.

5. For attribute-based issues use five questions for determining whether the person is coachable:

    Is the person taking ownership of the problem?

    Are they volunteering ideas for a solution?

    Do you sense any contrition?

    Are they willing to make compromises in their position to solve the problem?

    Are their fundamental values compatible with those of the organization?

6. For ethical lapses, ask whether the actions were indicative of who the person is (a pattern) or an exception.

7. Create a written development plan using concepts of IPF.

8. Avoid the set-up-to-fail syndrome by employing four concepts:
    a. you believe they can succeed;
    b. you want them to succeed;
    c. once corrected, the issue will not hang over them going forward;
    d. confidentiality.

9. Apply Sutton's *No Asshole Rule.*

Development Plan (DP)

It has been determined that your job performance requires attention for the following reasons:

```


```

This development plan (DP) is designed not as a reprimand, but as a *program* to correct a problem and get your career with us back on track. Make sure you fully understand the DP. The company *strongly* encourages you to check in with your supervisor during the DP period to make sure you understand how you are performing against the DP. You should understand that if you do not meet the objectives of this DP, you may be asked to leave.

You must correct these issues within 30/60 [circle one] days, or you will be subject to further action by the company. If at any time in the future your performance reflects the same problems outlined in this DP, you may be asked to leave without being placed on a new DP.

Your supervisor has designed the following required actions and changes. Make sure you read it carefully and understand what is involved. If you have any comments or objections, make those on this form before signing the DP.

```


```

After discussing the DP with your supervisor, if you have questions or concerns (including whether you are being treated fairly) discuss these issues immediately with your supervisor, their direct manager, or the personnel department. Do not wait until the conclusion of the DP to make your concerns known.

I (the employee) have the following comments or objections to this Development Plan:

Your signature indicates that you have received this DP, and that you have had the opportunity to express comments or objections.

_____   _____
Employee Name (printed)   Date

_____   _____
Employee Signature   Supervisor Signature

6 Breaking Up Is Hard to Do

There is overwhelming evidence that the higher the level of self-esteem, the more likely one will be to treat others with respect, kindness, and generosity.

—Nathaniel Brandon

My earliest difficult dismissal was the chief operating officer of the first company I ran. Let's call him Steven. I had plenty of excuses to keep him. The company was doing fine. We'd become friends. He worked diligently. We were hitting our plan, and our investors were happy. At the same time, we were not where we could be, and I knew in my heart that to get there we'd need a change in leadership. Nonetheless, I agonized for months.

Fortunately, when I came to the decision, I'd been coached on how to let someone go. Had I not, the process would have been harder on the company, but especially on Steven. When I delivered the news, he was professional about it, although distraught and embarrassed. We agreed on a smooth transition and a fair severance. I helped him in his new career where he started his own company. There he succeeded, and in a great twist of friendship and fate we became his biggest customer. Thirty years later, we're still in touch.

It's a reflection of our humanity that we postpone telling someone devastating news. But as Debra L. Dunn, vice president of strategy and corporate operations at Hewlett-Packard, explains, "There is no greater disrespect you can do to a person than to let them hang out in a job where they are not respected by their peers, not viewed as successful, and probably losing their self-esteem. To do that under the guise of respect for people is, to me, ridiculous."[1]

For the same reason we postpone our decision, we also often botch the process by trying to make it not hurt. There's no escaping that letting someone go is hard, just as Neil Sedaka put it in his number one hit song, "Breaking Up Is Hard to Do." And just like with our romantic break-ups, trying to make it easy on the other person almost always makes it harder for them.

Making the Decision

Most of us postpone the decision, hoping a more convenient time will come along. While there are seasonal situations and emergencies that require waiting, in the short term there is almost *never* a convenient time to dismiss an employee. A vacancy means additional workload for the remaining team, hiring a replacement, and a new onboarding process—all of which is time consuming. Yet, none of your problems will go away by procrastinating, and these are small prices to pay for the benefit of having the right long-term team in place.

Making the decision is tough, but if you've employed the subskills of these earlier chapters, you'll have applied the concepts of radical candor, provided them with instant performance feedback (IPF), offered results from 360 reviews, and given them a written development plan. If, after that, they still fail these four questions, it's likely necessary to ask them to leave:

Left Brain Check	*Ranking your team A, B, or C, where does this person come out?*
Right Brain Check	*If the person came into your office and resigned for a great opportunity, and provided a smooth transition, would you be relieved, neutral, or devastated?*
In 3 Years. . .	*Does this person have a place "on the bus" in three years?*
Would You Rehire. . .	*If you were filling a vacancy, would you hire this person for the same position for 125% of his or her current salary?*

When an employment relationship does not work out, generally both the employer and the employee share some responsibility. While you don't owe anyone a forever-job in a position they are not succeeding in, you do owe them a fair and benevolent transition to their next position. Ray Dalio, whom I introduced earlier, notes that the decision to procrastinate harms both parties: "Keeping a person in a job they are not suited for is terrible both for the person (because it prevents personal evolution) and our community (because we all bear the consequences, and it erodes meritocracy)."[2]

Preparation Is Compassion

In my course at Stanford, we practice dismissing an employee. I play the role of the employee being fired, and a student plays the manager. Playing the part of the employee, I ask what will happen to my health benefits. Most students respond with something such as, "I'm not sure . . . let me get back to you." I then ask about severance, if I can keep my laptop, how many vacation days I have left, and if I get paid for my unused sick days. It quickly becomes evident that their inadequate preparation is sending me home unsettled and anxious, which is why *preparation is compassion.*

Begin your preparation by determining what the employee is owed financially. In most jurisdictions, employees are entitled to any earned vacation and paid time off, incurred expenses, and payroll through their last day—all of which you should have prepared either for direct deposit or in a check to hand to them.

You'll probably need to offer COBRA benefits, which is the federal program to provide continuation of health coverage for employers with 20 or more employees and likely unknown to them. COBRA ensures that after employees leave the company, they will keep their health benefits. Make sure they know about this program and prepare the paperwork for them, along with a simple explanation.[3]

If your company offers profit sharing, retirement plans, or ownership programs, familiarize yourself with the key terms. Since the person you're about to dismiss will likely be overwhelmed and may forget the details, provide them with a written explanation of the consequences of their departure to these programs. If they are required to execute any paperwork, have the documents prepared in advance, filling in whatever you can for them.

If you're paying severance, it is your responsibility to design a package that is reasonable. Never make the mistake of asking employees, "What do you think is fair?" That puts the burden on them at an emotionally stressful moment in their lives. Instead, review your written policies and speak with your advisors, then determine the correct amount. I recommend you offer a generous sum that any reasonable employee would accept. That will help you avoid future litigation, ensure a smooth process, and eliminate the wear and tear on you and the organization if you were to find yourself in a dispute or stressful back-and-forth negotiation. Extended severance also helps people get to their next position with less economic distress, and you'll sleep better knowing you were fair and generous.

You may want to offer outplacement services. If so, have the details prepared, including contact information and the steps for employees to access the service. By doing so, you demonstrate that you're serious about your offer to help them find a new position.

Consider access and retention of confidential company information prior to the meeting. I once dismissed a senior executive who was preparing to leave the next day for an international trip. I was unable to immediately recover her laptop, which I suspected had evidence of malfeasance. In the 48 hours that it took me to recover the laptop, she had a professional service erase the hard drive, and there was a suggestion that she retained confidential company information.

Decide as well if you'd be willing to provide a job recommendation. Just because one person doesn't belong on your bus, that doesn't mean they can't find the bus that is right for them. You can provide a recommendation, even for those who you've let go, by first telling them:

> *For the right position, I want to help with a reference. If you are considering using me, contact me in advance. Based on the job description, I'll tell you what I'd be comfortable saying. If that response works for you, then give out my name so I can help you find a good fit with another company, otherwise I'm not likely to be a helpful reference.*

Some coworkers may need to be alerted to the situation in advance, for example to calculate the vacation pay or prepare certain documents. However, tell as few people as possible, as late in the process as possible, and only on a need-to-know basis. You don't want to unnecessarily ask people to keep secrets, and the imminent departure of a coworker is fodder for gossip. Letting people find out indirectly that they're about to lose their job, because you unnecessarily told others, is counter to the values you're communicating as a leader.

Transition Agreement

If you are providing compensation or services beyond what is legally required ("consideration"), you'll want a release of claims from the employee. The arrangement is simply: *We will provide severance and services that are not legally required. In return, you agree that this arrangement is fair and that you will not take the severance and services, then later sue the company.*

As part of a *transition agreement*, you may require that neither of you will say anything damaging about the other (*non-disparagement*), and that the released employee will not later hire certain members of your team or solicit certain customers (*non-solicitation*). Finally, you may use this agreement to put in place, or to reinforce, any understanding regarding confidentiality of company information.

I generally make the severance payments conditional on compliance with these terms, and ideally spread the payments over a longer period to increase the consequences if the other party does not comply. For example, if you are paying six weeks of salary in severance, you may consider paying that same amount over a 12-week period, which provides a longer incentive for the other person to stay true to the terms of your transition agreement.

Courts may view some terms of a contract signed during a dismissal as unenforceable out of the concern that they were entered into under duress or coercion. Address this by giving employees a few days to review what is being asked of them in the transition agreement.

Use clear and simple language and avoid the use of unnecessary legalese to reduce the chances of someone misunderstanding the transition agreement.

Legalese can also be intimidating and signal an adversarial relationship. For the same reason, encourage employees to get legal advice and highlight aspects of the agreement that may be averse to them, making clear in bold or underlined text that by signing the agreement, they lose the chance to later sue the company. My own experience has been that the more specific you are about this, the more likely the agreement will be enforced by third parties and the courts.

In some jurisdictions, employees may be allowed to change their minds after signing the transition agreement. This may be called the *period of recission*. For that reason, avoid making severance payments until this period has expired. After the period of recission has passed, have them sign a letter stating that they chose not to rescind the transition agreement so that there is no question as to the choice they made.

Be especially cautious about dismissing someone in a protected class. The Civil Rights Act of 1964 includes protection against discrimination in the workplace, specifying groups that have been historically discriminated against. In the United States, certain characteristics are included in protected classes such as: sex, race, age, disability, color, creed, national origin, religion, sexual orientation, whistleblowers, and genetic information. The consequences of incorrectly dismissing someone from a protected class can be substantial. The risk of litigation can cost well over $25,000 in the simplest cases, and much more with complex cases. This is not a reason to keep them on the bus, but instead to consult an expert prior to determining your implementation plan, and then by offering a transition agreement that both parties can agree is fair.

Breaking Up Is Hard to Do

If you are a kindhearted person, there is no way to make breaking up easy. Which is why struggling to knit the precise words together so that it won't be painful is unrealistic and will generally make things worse. Avoid any version of, "This is also hard for me," "I hope you can understand," or "I'd like to remain friends," which many of us have tried unsuccessfully in romantic breakups and are no more effective in a workplace breakup. Those pleas are about assuaging your feelings of guilt. But this moment is not about you, and you have to accept the consequences that come from leadership and the hard stuff that comes with a *commitment to building a great team.*

Directness is kindness. The meeting should last less than 10 minutes. Avoid opening with any small talk; the person will see from your face that bad news is coming, and any delay only increases the awkwardness and their discomfort:

> *Caleb, I'm sorry but I've come to the decision that this is no longer a good fit. You belong at a place where you can excel with the talents you have. As difficult as this will be, I now need to go over the terms of your transition . . .*

Do not mistake ambiguous terms with benevolence. My Stanford colleague, Jim Ellis, who cofounded the billion-dollar company Asurion, writes about a manager at Gillette who told a person he was being "moved out" because the manager didn't want to use more specific language in a misdirected attempt at kindness. As a result, for well into the meeting the employee thought he was just being transferred to another position.

You may be tempted to justify your decision or to get the other person to agree with you—especially if you are pressed by them for the reasons behind your decision. That will often turn into a debate, and before you know it, you will find yourself making a stronger and stronger case for their deficiencies, leaving that person feeling miserable and broken. It might seem unfair to not explain the specifics behind your choice, but the person has been handed terrible news and their mind is flooded with emotions, possibly of anger, embarrassment, and resentment. They may be worried about what to say to their spouse or partner, whether they need to cancel their planned vacation, and how they will find another job. They're in no mental state to digest performance feedback. Which is why if they ask for the reasons they're being asked to leave the team, I generally say:

> *I'd like to give you whatever specifics you might find helpful. If you want to set a time to go over the reasons for my decision, we can do so. I'll come prepared and with notes. I suggest sometime next week after we come to an agreement on the terms of your separation. But the purpose of this meeting is to go over the terms of your separation.*

If they press you for more information, return to the phrase: "The purpose of this meeting is to go over the terms of your separation," and repeat the offer to have a separate meeting. If they insist that you're not being fair by not going into the details, stay firm knowing you're showing them compassion and kindness by not going into the specifics in that meeting. Then move to the details of the separation agreement.

Finally, take personal responsibility for the decision rather than spreading responsibility to others. Don't deflect onto your boss, the owners, the board of directors, or any other constituent. You made the decision; you need to own it.

Logistics

Experienced managers have different opinions on the best day of the week to have the meeting. I prefer Fridays as it gives the employee the weekend to process the information. For most, Saturday and Sunday are not workdays. They're not immediately facing an unexpected empty day, as they would if they were suddenly home on a weekday. I've also found the weekend to be a good cooling off period, where they may regain perspective on the situation.

I don't find it necessary to have other people in the room as witnesses, and I find it unnecessarily harsh. Andrea Jung is the former chief executive officer of Avon and board member of Apple, Unilever, and Wayfair. She and I have talked extensively about this issue, and we both agree that including a witness implies distrust and unnecessarily subjects the person to an audience. Our shared experience is that the best protection from accusations of wrongful discharge is in following the laws within your jurisdiction and in getting agreement on a fair and thorough transition agreement.[4]

Try to meet in a windowless office or conference room to avoid the chance of other employees observing what should be a private meeting. Some managers choose to dismiss their employees off-site, but this can be logistically problematic as they'll need to return to retrieve personal possessions, likely in front of others, at a moment in time when they'd probably prefer a fast departure.

Be prepared for various emotional responses. The first time a person broke down after I presented the news, I watched uncomfortably not knowing what else to do. That created an embarrassing situation for them, which I regret to this day. Breakdowns happen. Have a bottle of water and tissues available. If someone is overcome, consider an excuse to leave the room for a few minutes to allow them to regroup in private and regain their dignity.

The end of the day is the best time to have the meeting, ideally after as many coworkers as possible have gone home. The walk out of the building is upsetting and possibly embarrassing, and the fewer people they must see or speak with generally the better. Some companies have employees escorted out of the building by security, but as Andrea and I have experienced, in almost all cases it is unnecessary and humiliating, and it implies that absent a security guard, the person would do something dangerous or improper—which is rarely the case.

In extraordinary situations, employees may become disruptive, perhaps expressing powerful negative feelings about you or the company to other team members. If this happens, gracefully accelerate their departure, but with an eye to avoiding an escalation—even if it means allowing them more time to say and act negatively. While I have no way to measure the risk someone may face in any particular dismissal, my own experience has been that the company recovered from those few difficult minutes faster than if an escalation led to requiring force to remove the employee, or the escalation led to violence.[5]

Communication to Employees

Limit comments to the remaining team to what they need to know in order to resume their work. This preserves the privacy of the most impacted person and reassures your team that if the situation were reversed, they would not become the subject of gossip. There will be exceptions, such as when someone has stolen company property or if the dismissal has material implications to the business. But in most cases the reasons for someone's departure are not anyone else's business.

The implications of their departure, however, are their business. Begin with the following script:

> As you know, Sharon is no longer with the company. The specific reasons are between the two of us, and out of respect we're not going to make her departure a source of rumor or gossip, which is inconsistent with our values. However, there are several issues that are specific to your work going forward, and I'd like to address those now . . . .

As you do so, four legitimate questions are likely on your employees' minds:

> How will the person's current work get done?
>
> Do you plan to replace the person, and by when?
>
> How will this impact any reporting relationships?
>
> Will you be considering internal candidates?

Don't wait for them to request answers to these questions. Doing so leaves the remaining team to reach their own conclusions, and it detracts from your brand as a manager. What they want to know is that you have a thoughtful plan in place, and that the company's future is secure.

A Final Thought . . .

Prior to teaching at Stanford, Joel Peterson had run the largest real estate firm in the world, and when he wasn't teaching at Stanford, he was busy as JetBlue's chairman and founding investor. For years, Joel and I taught a course together, and one lesson I learned from Joel was understanding that letting people go is part of a leader's job description. As Joel puts it:

> The best leaders are just as good at removing people from jobs for which they're unsuited as they are at putting rising stars into the right positions. It isn't possible to be error-free in hiring—and even if it were, organizations change, roles shift, and you may find that even highly skilled employees can't adapt.[6]

If you want to build a great team, there is no getting around this aspect of your job description. Anyone who tells me they have never let someone go isn't showing evidence of superhuman hiring ability, but a lack of commitment to building a winning team. If you're committed to excellent leadership, you'll have to accept this unpleasant aspect of the job of manager.

Breaking Up Is Hard to Do

1. Before dismissing someone, ask yourself whether you have applied the subskills of IPF, 360 reviews, and coaching underperformance.

2. In making your decision, ask yourself four questions from Chapter 5 (Coaching Underperformance):

    How would I rank the team member: A, B, or C?

    If the person resigned, would I be relieved or devastated?

    "In three years . . ." what does my organization chart look like?

    "If I were filling a vacancy, knowing what I know today, would I hire this person for the same position at 125% his/her current salary?"

3. Preparation is compassion:
    a. Prepare a check for any earned vacation and paid time off, incurred expenses, and payroll through their last day.
    b. Disclose and prepare paperwork for health benefit continuation (COBRA).
    c. Prepare paperwork for profit sharing, retirement plans, ownership programs, and other benefits.
    d. Provide details on any outplacement services.
    e. Have a plan to recover confidential information and company property.

4. Prepare a transition agreement and have it prepared in advance of the meeting:
    a. Determine what severance will be offered.
    b. Pay severance over time, not in a lump sum.
    c. Consider a non-solicitation and non-disparagement clause.

    d. Use clear and simple language.

    e. Give them time to review the material with any advisors they may have.

    f. Understand any recission rights in your state. After the period of recission, have them acknowledge in writing that they have not chosen to rescind the agreement.

5. Tell as few people as possible, as late in the process as possible, on a need-to-know basis.

6. Be direct in your communication. Keep the meeting short.

7. Focus on the terms of their departure, not the reasons for their departure. Offer to have a separate meeting if they would like details of the reasons for their dismissal.

8. Manage the logistics to limit their embarrassment with other employees (windowless office, at the end of the day, preferably a Friday). Have tissues and water at hand.

9. Focus your communication to the remaining employees on four issues:

    How will the person's current work get done?

    Do you plan to replace the person, and by when?

    How will this impact any reporting relationships?

    Will you be considering internal candidates?

Nothing in this book or in the example of a transition agreement is intended to suggest legal advice or workplace risk management. The material presented does not suggest any specific course of action regarding legal matters, assessing the risk of violence, or responding to a potentially violent situation. I am not a lawyer, nor am I an authority in risk management or assessing and responding to workplace violence. I am only conveying what I have come to understand through my experience. The material offers general information and does not address any specific suggestion on how you might handle your situation, nor does it offer any guidance involving a particular set of facts or provide advice on how you might proceed. Nothing in this book implies an attorney–client relationship.

Model Transition Agreement

[Date]

Mrs. Julie Jacobs

11825 Saint Sebastian Blvd.

Tulsa, Oklahoma

Dear Julie:

This letter will confirm arrangements for a special payment package being offered to you as a result of your dismissal with _____ ("Company") effective _____. For the purpose of this agreement, the definition of Company includes its officers, directors, shareholders, and affiliated organizations.

In consideration of your agreement to, and compliance with, the terms contained in this letter and all exhibits, Company will provide you with the compensation described below. The compensation described will be paid to you provided you acknowledge your agreement with the terms outlined in this letter and otherwise comply with the obligations listed below and attached in Exhibit A.

1. You will receive a payment equal to _____ weeks at your current salary level, paid out over a _____ week period through the regular payroll. All payments under this paragraph will be subject to normal and customary deductions and withholdings.

2. You further agree that, unless under legal compulsion, you will not in any way or at any other time intentionally communicate to any party anything that would be derogatory in nature about the Company, its business, or reputation.

3. For a period of _____ weeks, we will make available to you reasonable administrative support to assist you in securing employment elsewhere.

(continued)

4. You understand that failure on your part to comply with all of the terms of this agreement (including paragraph 2) may result in the termination of this agreement (including paragraphs 1 and 3).

5. You understand that the terms of this agreement and the attached release are contingent upon the execution of Exhibit A and that you do not revoke such execution of Exhibit A (although you have certain rights to do so).

6. In consideration of the above (including but not limited to paragraphs 1 and 3), the receipt of which you acknowledge, you release and discharge the Company from any and all claims arising from your employment (including claims to compensation, bonus, or equity rights but excluding vested retirement benefits such as 401(K)) and claims of discrimination and wrongful discharge.

7. You have been given this agreement on _____. You acknowledge that you have been given at least 21 days to consider this agreement. During this period, you may seek advice from a lawyer. For this agreement to be effective, you must sign it in the presence of a witness and return the agreement to _____.

You have 7 days after you return the signed agreement to cancel it. This agreement will not become effective and enforceable until after this 7-day period expires. If you choose to cancel this agreement, you must send written notice to Company attention: _____ and state, "I hereby revoke my acceptance of our letter agreement and attached release." If you do not wish to revoke this agreement, 7 days after your execution of this agreement please sign the attached form and send it to _____.

YOU UNDERSTAND THAT BY ACCEPTING THE TERMS OF THIS AGREEMENT, AND BY SIGNING THIS LETTER, YOU ARE RELINQUISHING ANY RIGHT TO SUE COMPANY OR ITS DIRECTORS, OFFICERS, AND EMPLOYEES, ON THE BASIS OF SUCH CLAIM OR HAVE ANY ACTION FILED ON YOUR BEHALF AGAINST THE COMPANY.

You acknowledge that this release is made by you voluntarily and you acknowledge that you have been given the opportunity to review your options and are encouraged to consult with advisors of your choosing, including an attorney, prior to signing this letter of release.

You also acknowledge that you have had an opportunity to make changes or modifications to this agreement and have declined to do so. Agreed to and acknowledged:

_____   _____
Employee Name (printed)   Date

_____   _____
Employee Signature   Supervisor Signature

Exhibit A

This release is signed in conjunction with the letter agreement dated _____ to which this release is attached. You understand that in order for you to receive the compensation package described in the letter agreement, you must agree to the following general release:

In exchange for the consideration listed in the letter agreement, you agree to release and discharge Company from all legal claims which you ever had, or now have, as of the date of your signing this release. You promise not to sue Company or to start any legal proceedings against Company arising out of your employment by Company, ending of your employment by Company, and the actions described in this letter. This includes but is not limited to, for example, any legal claims based on any of the following laws:

Title VII of the Civil Rights Act

The Employee Retirement Income Security Act

The Immigration Reform and Control Act

The Americans with Disabilities Act

The Consolidated Omnibus Budget Reconciliation Act of 1985

(continued)

The Age Discrimination in Employment Act

The Older Workers Benefit Protection Act

The Occupational Safety and Health Act

The National Labor Relations Act

The Fair Labor Standards Act

The Civil Rights Act of 1866

The Civil Rights Act of 1991

Title 42 U.S.C. Section 1981 through 1988, inclusive

The Rehabilitation Act

The Equal Pay Act

Family and Medical Leave Act

The Worker Adjustment and Retraining Notification Act

The Immigration Control and Reform Act any other federal, state, or local civil rights or anti-discrimination law, defamation, wrongful discharge, negligent infliction of emotional distress, intentional infliction of emotional distress, and misrepresentation any local, state, or federal law, regulation, or ordinance and or public policy, contract, or tort law.

By signing this agreement, you also waive any right or interest you may now have or have had in reinstatement.

You acknowledge that this agreement is made by you voluntarily and you acknowledge that you have been given the opportunity to review your options and consult with advisors of your choosing, including an attorney, prior to signing this letter of release. You also acknowledge that you have had an opportunity to make changes or modifications to this agreement and have declined to do so.

If you do not sign this release, you will not receive any of the benefits or compensation outlined in the letter agreement. If you choose to revoke this release after you have signed it, you will lose all the benefits and compensation described above, and you will also have to pay back any benefits or compensation that you have received under the letter agreement.

(continued)

You further understand that if, within 9 days after entering into this agreement, we do not receive the letter stating that you have elected NOT to revoke this agreement, the benefits outlined in this agreement will be suspended until such time as we receive the letter.

I have read this release as well as the letter that it is attached to and agree with the terms described:

_____   _____
Employee Name (printed)   Date

_____
Employee Signature

_____   _____
Witness Name (printed)   Date

_____
Witness Signature

Mr. Roger Roberts

CEO, Fine Company, Inc.

438 21st Street

Tulsa, Oklahoma

HAND DELIVERED

Dear Mr. Roberts:

I have not revoked my acceptance of the compensation package outlined in the letter by Roger Roberts, dated _____ and signed by me on _____.

Cordially,

_____

7 Never Waste a Last Goodbye

The British nation is unique in this respect: they are the only people who like to be told how bad things are.

—Winston Churchill

I was once on the board of a healthcare company that was reporting unusually high turnover. The CEO said it was a function of a tight job market, and in response, the company needed to pay people higher wages. But after almost a year of losing good people while raising pay, the board asked me to conduct exit interviews with a handful of people who had recently turned in their resignations.

I learned that none of the people I spoke with were leaving to chase a higher salary. The reason for their discontent was that the CEO had created an intimidating work environment. But instead of dismissing the CEO, we curated the information in a form that would maximize the chances the CEO would accept and act on the information. It was a hard pill to swallow, and to his credit, he embraced the feedback and made lasting adjustments. Within a year, turnover dropped, and he went on to build a large and successful business. But the earlier cost to the organization was undeniable and could have been avoided had the company used the subskill of *exit interviews*.

A Competitive Weapon

In today's highly competitive labor market, the exit interview is one of the easiest ways to improve your ability to attract and retain great people. The best news of all is that most of your competition will be too insecure to take advantage of this subskill, making exit interviews a potent weapon in your competitive arsenal. Nationally, 26.3% of US workers leave their jobs each year, and the cost of turnover is estimated at a trillion dollars annually.[1] Yet a whopping 52% of employees who leave an organization report that their manager could have done something to prevent their departure,[2] and just over half of the people who leave report that no one asked them how they felt about the job or the company prior to their departure.[3]

Dr. Noelle Nelson observes in her book, *Make More Money by Making Your Employees Happy*, "When employees feel that the company takes their interest to heart, then the employees will take company interests to heart." This is backed up with data showing that *Fortune's* "100 Best Companies to Work For" had an average annual stock rise of more than twice that of the overall market.[4] Furthering the case that exit interviews are a competitive weapon, in one of his articles on personal and workplace happiness, Arthur Brooks of the Harvard Business School cites Gallup data that show that more than three-quarters of companies in the highest percentile of employee engagement outperform their competition.[5]

Departing employees generally have little to lose by revealing information that they may have previously been reluctant to disclose. Through an exit interview, you may learn that your employees are considering unionizing or that they feel misled by the recent rollout of the new health plan. Someone on the way out might report that an executive is stealing from you or that your vice president of marketing has been interviewing for other positions. There is an almost limitless catalog of information available during a well-managed exit interview.

Despite the clear use case, many managers avoid instituting a system of exit interviews because often—deep down—they fear what employees might say. That was true in my case. I preferred my own narrative whenever someone left my organization. It's easier. Not wanting to take responsibility for my role in losing a great employee, I wrote the story I wanted to tell. All of which may be normal, but as the leadership expert Ken Blanchard says, "Feedback is the breakfast of champions."[6]

There's no denying the gruel of feedback can be hard to digest at times. Nonetheless, if you're willing to choke it down, there is no question you'll increase your chances of becoming a champion. It's an act of personal and organizational vulnerability to create a process where a person who has decided to break up with you—or with whom you just broke up—has the chance to "tell all." Yet it's important to know what happened and what can be done to improve the organization—and you generally get only one chance to hear from your star witness.

The Interviewer

It is a mistake to conduct exit interviews with managers who are untrained or who lack the necessary attributes to conduct an exit interview. The interviewer must unearth information hidden beneath company politics and social norms. The insights from an exit interview must be carefully mined by someone who can create an environment where the employee feels comfortable revealing awkward or sensitive information, which makes choosing and training the interviewer the most critical element in the process.

Interviewers must be good at active listening and able to convey trustworthiness. They should have a reputation for avoiding company politics. For departing employees to open up, they need to believe the interviewer holds a position within the organizational structure that allows them to speak truth to power. Otherwise, they'll wonder if their comments will matter.

To remain objective, interviewers should not have a direct reporting relationship with the employee or the employee's manager, and it's also best that the CEO not participate in the interview. Former employees need the chance to reveal issues about the company's leadership and be able to make observations such as, "People think she's in over her head," which would be hard for someone to say directly to the person.

The selected person will also need direct access to the company's legal counsel and board of directors in the rare case they come across sensitive information that involves misconduct within the leadership team. If your organization is large enough, a senior person in human resources is a prime candidate. Alternatively, consider using a paid outside resource such as an executive coach or contract HR firm.

The Interview

The ideal time for an exit interview is the employee's last day of employment. Some managers believe waiting several weeks later affords employees greater perspective, but, as time goes on, they are likely to have a lesser stake in your organization and may forget important details. It also gets harder to arrange time with them once they're busy with the next chapter in their lives.

Interviews should take place at the end of the day, after subjects have completed their work responsibilities. Since you can't be sure where the conversation will go, schedule only a start time, with capacity on your calendar to allow for a longer meeting.

Interviewers should position their role as a curious team member, treating departing employees as subject matter experts. They should begin by demonstrating an openness to new ideas and reassuring the departing team member that the purpose of the meeting is not to preserve the status quo:

> We know there are always areas for improvement. This is our chance to become a better company. It's also why I'm doing this interview, to make it as easy as possible for you to be frank and candid.

Interviewers cannot promise confidentiality. There are considerations beyond their control, for example if someone's safety is at risk. However, a promise of discretion often suffices:

> I can't promise not to repeat anything you say, since I don't know what you are about to tell me. For example, if someone's safety is at risk, I'll have to address that. But I will promise that I'll use discretion, and if there is anything that you want treated in a special way, tell me beforehand and we'll try to find an accommodation.

Never substitute forms, surveys, and numerical ratings for an exit interview. Strive for a structured conversation, featuring open-ended questions. Exclude "yes" or "no" from the possible responses. For instance, rather than ask . . .

> *Is there anything concerning that we need to know about Catalina's management style?*

. . . which could be answered as "yes" or "no," consider an open-ended question:

> *What about Catalina's management style is getting in the way of her success, which if she knew about it would help her become a better manager?*

Note how the question I just modeled is not framed to tattle on Catalina, but to collect information that Catalina would want to know.

The person nonetheless may be reluctant to speak, which is why interviewers should be comfortable with pauses and silence as the other person assembles their words, or the courage, to say what is on their mind. In cases where people are especially reluctant to offer information, the interviewer can demonstrate that the process is a gift to their former coworkers whom they may still have affection and loyalty toward:

> *Lilly, I'm glad you had a good experience with Catalina, but none of us are above finding ways to improve. I know Catalina wants to improve and will be grateful for your guidance. But also, this is your chance to help your coworkers like Gabriel and Rashid, who will benefit from Catalina's development as a manager.*

Interviewers should also ask about any workplace issues that may require resolution. In such cases—for instance, an unreimbursed expense report or an unmet corporate commitment—the interviewer should find out whether the employee received satisfaction with a simple question: *Was the issue resolved?*

If the employee was dismissed and it's possible to do an exit interview, the interviewer should focus on the deficits and opportunities the employee sees for the company. Avoid discussing the reasons for dismissal, unless they believe that they have a legal basis for a wrongful termination, such as a retaliation or discrimination—which you will want to know.

The Three Cs

Similar to what can happen in a confidential 360 process, departing employees may use the interview for reprisal by saying nasty things, and they may also word helpful comments poorly. An exit interview is not the equivalent of a message board to post raw data or complaints, which is why you should apply the *three Cs* before you discuss your findings with anyone: *curate* the feedback; *create* a personal growth plan that addresses *obstacles, support,* and *alignment;* and *close* the loop with the impacted person. The best output from an exit interview is a personal growth plan that uses the tools for 360 reviews and instant performance feedback to make meaningful improvements to your organization.

The purpose of the curation is to make the information more useful by eliminating phrases or references that degrade the actionable information. Like the 360 process, the interviewer's task is to sort out irrelevant or ill-intentioned comments and find nuggets that, when corroborated with evidence, will be useful to coworkers or the company. While not every exit interview produces new information, reinforcing and confirming existing beliefs are also helpful to you as a manager.

A Final Thought . . .

Phil Seefried cofounded a highly successful investment bank. In an industry with notoriously high turnover, his firm was able to cut its turnover rate to almost nothing, in part by employing exit interviews to continuously adjust his culture, norms, and processes. But Seefried went a step further—a *pre-exit interview*. Every year, senior management would ask their employees two simple questions: "Why do you stay here?" and "What would it take for you to leave?" In doing so, they were able to better identify problems *before* they occurred, and deal with issues that might cost them a great team member.

The use of a pre-exit interview was one of the reasons why Seefried's company continually appeared on his industry's "Best Place to Work" lists.

Never Waste a Last Goodbye

1. Attributes of a good interviewer include the following:
   a. Active listener
   b. Conveys trustworthiness
   c. In a position that allows them to speak truth to power
   d. No reporting relationship with the employee's manager
   e. Not the CEO

2. Conduct the interview on the employee's last day of employment, at the end of the day, after their responsibilities have been completed.

3. Demonstrate an openness to new ideas and reassure them that the purpose is not to preserve the status quo.

4. You cannot promise confidentiality; however, a promise of discretion often suffices.

5. Strive for a structured conversation, featuring open-ended questions that reveal critical information.

6. Ask questions that exclude "yes" or "no" from the possible responses.

7. Never substitute an exit interview with forms and numerical ratings.

8. Apply the three Cs:
   a. *Curate* the feedback, summarizing general themes rather than raw comments.
   b. *Create* a personal growth plan that addresses *obstacles, support,* and *alignment.*
   c. *Close* the loop.

9. Consider a pre-exit interview process to understand why people stay and what it would take for them to leave.

Ten Exit Interview Questions

1. What ultimately led you to accept the new position?

2. What would have changed your mind about leaving?

3. How would you describe the culture of our company?

4. What would make this a better place for people to work?

5. What about this company would you recommend to friends?

6. What are the biggest risks for our company that you see?

7. What did you like the best, and least, about your job?

8. Did you receive constructive feedback to help you improve your performance?

9. Did you feel your manager gave you what you needed to succeed?

10. If you owned this company, what would you want to make the leadership aware of that you don't think they know?

PART II
Fanatical
Custodian of Time

8 Activity Is Not Progress

It's not enough to be busy. So are the ants. The question is, what are we busy about?

—Henry David Thoreau

For years, I'd spend each week getting further behind, then try to catch up over the weekend. When Monday arrived, I assumed the upcoming week would be different, that I'd get to the important work, see more of my daughters, miss no more dinners at home, and use that gym membership. But each week was like the one that came before it.

What I failed to understand was that as the size of my organization increased, so too did the demands on my time. More people wanted my attention while my own priorities were pushed to the sidelines. I found myself responding to more emails and requests by people who wanted to "pick my brain." Ironically, the technology that promised to improve my situation made things worse: my smartphone became a leash as I could be reached at any time, on any day, by just about anyone. People expected me to read my email 24/7, and through the internet almost anyone could dig up my email address. Sites like LinkedIn gave everyone permission to cold call me; calendar apps allowed people to schedule time on my calendar without asking; and video technology made it too easy to schedule hour-long meetings to cover 20-minute topics.

I tried to muscle through this technology thicket—starting each morning with a promise to be more present with my children, not incessantly check email, attend fewer meetings, and be better at saying no. But emergencies erupted. Team members knocked on my door with the dreaded words, "Got a minute?" The important proposal that I needed to complete shifted onto the weekend calendar. Low-value activity ceaselessly filled whatever time I'd created for my own priorities.

My frustration came to an end one afternoon. Over coffee on the Stanford campus, I asked my friend Tom Staggs how he managed a team of more than 200,000 employees with the same number of hours in the day as I had. At the time, Tom was chief operating officer of the Walt Disney Company, running an organization that was orders of magnitude larger than mine, while he still had the same hours in the day as me.

He explained how in order to do so, he had to be an especially careful custodian of his most precious and finite resource: his time. As long as I let other people set my agenda, he said, I didn't have a chance. After that coffee, I observed the time-management habits of other leadership superheroes, and I read what they had to say about how they too protected their time. I came to realize that Tom was right. One of the five lessons from people that got things done is the extent to which they protect their time.

Start by Creating Quantity

Frank Gilbreth may be best known for his role in the book *Cheaper by the Dozen*. In it, he humorously describes how to feed 12 children and get them off to school every day. But before the famous book, Gilbreth made a name for himself as an expert in scientific management. In his most recognized work, he showed that by raising stacks of bricks to chest level, bricklayers could set twice the number of bricks in the same amount of time.[1] In a modern-day example, my Stanford colleagues Robert Sutton and Huggy Rao describe in their bestselling book, *Scaling up Excellence*,[2] how techniques as esoteric as whether to coil an air hose in a figure-eight versus a circle reduces the average NASCAR pit stop from 22 seconds to 20 seconds (which matters in races often won by tenths of a second).

For a century following Gilbreth's work, industrial engineering permeated nearly every aspect of the workplace except one: management. What we know today is that managers can create more quantity of time, about two hours each day, by applying a version of the same techniques once used to get a dozen children off to school or to speed a car through a pit stop.

Compress Your Meeting Times

About 4,000 years ago, the Babylonians divided the day into increments divisible with the number 12—which they calculated by multiplying their four fingers with the three joints in each.[3] That's right, the number of joints in your hand is why 30 and 60 minutes is the default time for nearly every meeting in the world.

Not wanting to let dead Babylonian mathematicians run my calendar, I tried an experiment, reducing the length of my one-hour meetings to 40 minutes, and my half-hour meetings to 20 minutes. This may not seem like much, but managers spend a whopping 72% of their work hours in meetings.[4] Based on my own historical work schedule, that one simple adjustment added 70 minutes of time to each day—or close to an entire additional day each week!

And there were two bonuses that I did not anticipate. First, those unconventional time frames conveyed a message that the meetings should begin and end on time. It turns out that when a meeting is scheduled to end at 10:20, people assume there's a reason. People showed up on time, and we got right down to business. We got more work done in those 20-minute meetings than we did in the previous 30-minute meetings. The second bonus is that fewer meetings ran five to ten minutes over. These changes, taken together, saved me 80 minutes per day.

The OHIO Rule

The *OHIO Rule* stands for: *Only Handle It Once*. The average amount of time a manager spends on a single event is just over three minutes, and on average, they engage with 12.2 different working spheres in a single day, switching every 10 minutes from one task to the next.[5] This practice is described by neuroscientists as *task switching*, and we know it is an inefficient way to complete work.

Take for example one study where researchers gave participants two assignments. One group had to complete building a model log cabin, and afterward respond to a set of text and email messages. The other group was told to respond to the same messages, but to do so immediately as they arrived on their phone. The first group responded to all the messages, and completed building the log cabin, in about one-third less time.

The study reminded me of a meeting I had with someone whose plane had arrived late. When she landed, she apologized for not alerting me by email but said that the flight's internet was inoperable. She then admitted that while she was sorry that she couldn't contact me, she got a ton of work done as a result. With no internet to distract her, she increased her intensity of focus (worked faster) and reduced the leakage from task switching.

This is all because our brains can't switch from one task to another instantly. We need a moment to reorient before fully engaging in the subsequent work. There is a cognitive ramp-up required each time we begin work on a task. Attention focused on the prior activity remains present as we shift into another activity. As we toggle between assignments, we pay this cognitive toll, referred to by researchers as the *residual effect*. Like the woman on the airplane, you've no doubt also experienced how much faster you complete your work when you don't incessantly stop and start—now you know why.

There is no getting around the residual effect. This is how we are cognitively wired, and self-discipline can't alter how the human brain works. Chipping away at a single task over multiple times throughout the day requires more minutes than doing it all at once. But the cost is even higher than wasting the quantity of time you have. When you focus on a single task, your concentration and energy moves at an accelerated pace. Task switching lessens the intensity at which we address the work, hence not just increasing the time we need to complete the work, but also decreasing the speed at which we do the work. OHIO is like having only half as far to go, while traveling at twice the speed.

The reason we task switch, and why it's hard to stop, is because cognition behaves like a muscle and gets fatigued. At the earliest excuse, our brain asks for a break in the same way an athlete wants to skip the last five push-ups in practice. Crossing off a few emails, signing approvals, reading an article that flashed on the screen is easy work. It is a lower cognitive load and is the brain's version of taking a water break instead of completing those last five push-ups. But since we don't want to admit that's what is happening, we tell ourselves that reading a humdrum email counts as work, even though in reality we're just taking a break.

Understanding that task switching is about cognitive fatigue was the revelation I needed to embrace OHIO. I set milestones, such as how many minutes I'll work on something before taking a break—much like I might set the number of push-ups to complete—regardless of how much my brain complains.

Our brains do need a recovery period, just like other muscles. However, instead of task switching, which doesn't provide for much relief, when I take a break I do something that requires almost no concentration. I'll close my eyes for 10 minutes, take a walk, or do the dishes. I get a faster recovery this way and can return to my important work sooner and fresher.

Be Excellent at Saying "No"

A friend of mine who ran a software company in Boston was interested in learning more about West Coast venture capital. He asked me if he could meet a Stanford colleague of mine who ran a prominent venture capital firm. To my surprise, my colleague declined. I was initially put off by his response. But his position reflected what Tom Staggs had tried to explain to me that afternoon at Stanford. High-performing leaders don't feel the requirement to read every article someone sends them, reply to every unsolicited LinkedIn message, or have breakfast with someone just because a Stanford colleague asks them. As a busy venture capitalist, if my colleague responded to every request for a meeting to "pick his brain," he'd have no time to work on the priorities that mattered to him.

Saying "no" does not always mean you can't help the other person at all. Instead of an hour-long lunch, suggest a 20-minute cup of coffee. They get what they need, while you save a valuable 40 minutes. Since I'm often asked the same questions by my students, and I end up offering essentially the same response, I now first send a paper with background information. We have a shorter call, but one that has higher impact and value to them.

Not only is it okay to say "no," in a polite form, to be a high-performing leader you must learn to do so. It can be uncomfortable at times, and some people are put off when you decline (as I was with my Stanford colleague). But that is not a reason to give out your scarcest resource without intention. As Lou Gerstner, the former chief executive officer of IBM, once said, "Never let anyone own your schedule."

Then Create Quality

For months, whenever I sent an email to my friend Katherine Gehl, I'd get an autoreply: "I'm sorry but I'm working on an important project and won't be able to respond to your email." Katherine formerly ran a large family-owned company—if you ever had nachos and cheese at a ballgame, it was probably produced by Gehl Foods. But she had since sold the business and was running the Institute for Political Innovation, which addresses our floundering political system.

When I asked Katherine about the email reply, she explained that she was working on a book.[6] The book was her priority, and she believed that the people important to her would understand. She then was kind enough to send me a copy of *Deep Work* by Cal Newport, a computer science professor at Georgetown University.[7] What struck me was Newport's distinction between *shallow work* and *deep work*. Shallow work refers to simple tasks that require little in the way of concentration and add limited value. Shallow work can be done in almost any environment and in short windows of time. Deep work is where creativity and innovation takes place, such as writing a book on political innovation, but requires uninterrupted periods of concentration.

Interruptions in your day increase attention residue. Similar to the residual effect, attention residue is the condition whereby whatever you worked on most recently intrudes on the next task. After you finish responding to a complaint from an important customer, that occupies a portion of your attention, and it will take time before the customer complaint is no longer in your cognitive sphere. Because you're involuntarily toggling back and forth, your deep work is receiving only a portion of your attention, leaving you less creative and working at a slower pace.

This is one of the reasons that deep work cannot be performed if it's wedged between responding to emails, hallway conversations, and trips for coffee. Making travel plans, knocking out simple emails, and approving routine decisions are a necessary part of getting through life, but they can take place in almost any environment. Deep work requires a deliberate setting of uninterrupted time, generally several hours, and in the next chapter I describe skills for doing just that.

We are drawn to shallow work because it is easy and falsely satisfying. Yet our most important work usually comes from deep work, such as preparing a performance review, designing a new commission plan, planning a customer presentation, or reviewing a product proposal—where success is the *quality* of the output, not the *quantity*.

Transactional emails need to be answered and hotel reservations must be made. But Newport demonstrates that without guardrails, shallow work consumes our attention and elbows out our time for deep work. In a perfect example of institutionalizing deep work within an organization, I recently came across a paper describing a software company that banned coworker interruptions on Tuesdays, Thursdays, and Fridays so its engineers would have more time to write code. That policy increased productivity from 47% to 65%.[8]

Know Your Chronotype

Chronotype is a term psychologists use to describe an individual's inclination to sleep and wake up at a certain time. It also determines when you are best suited for different tasks, including deep versus shallow work.

During the day our body temperature, blood pressure, and melatonin level fluctuates based on circadian rhythms, age, gender, and genetics. It's why some people work best at night, while others fare better in the morning. By knowing your chronotype, you can use your nature to your advantage. If you don't know your chronotype, there are scientific questionnaires that can help you make that determination.[9]

If you drag toward the end of the day, schedule shallow work for the afternoons, and preserve mornings for creative work. While it can be satisfying in the moment to see the content of your inbox disappear, don't waste your best circadian energy paying your credit card bill. Determine what time of day you are most alert, focused, and creative, and then block out as much of that time for deep work. In my case, I block out deep work for the morning. My assistant knows to not schedule meetings then, if possible, and packs administrative work, or work that requires little to any creativity, into the afternoon when my cognitive skills are weaker and fatigued.

Change Your Environment

Two years ago, I decided to stop eating Milk Duds before I went to bed. I love the taste at the end of the day, but the caffeine and sugar disrupted my sleep. I tried to cut back, but with limited success. Night after night I'd come up with a new excuse and grab a handful of Milk Duds, only to wake the next morning disappointed at my poor self-control. Promises to change and improve were easy, but the daily temptations pulled me back like an enormous rubber band.

If I wanted to eat fewer Milk Duds, I needed to control my environment. B.J. Fogg, the director of the Behavior Design Lab at Stanford University and stand-out author of *Tiny Habits*,[10] explains, "There's just one way to radically change your behavior: radically change your environment." In one triumphant moment of self-control, I tossed out the stacked boxes of Milk Duds, and asked Wendy to stop buying any more. I've been Milk Dud sober for two years, but if she ever puts a box in the pantry, I'll be back at them.

We're no different in our work habits. Exposed to temptations, we eat chocolate at bedtime, respond to every request for our time, and let easy low-value work interrupt the work that adds value to our organization. For example, since I find my desk brings too many distractions, I sit in a separate place when I'm in my deep work time block, and like tossing out the Milk Duds, I leave my phone elsewhere. If I don't control my environment, those temptations chip away at my time, and I don't have a chance.

A Final Thought . . .

Almost every company sets restrictions on how conventional assets and resources can be used. Yet they seldom set a standard for their most critical resource: their manager's time. Which is why, once you become a fanatical custodian of your own time, you should instill these same habits and practices among your entire team. Imagine the power you create, for example, when your whole team, not just you, has an extra 70 minutes in their day as they carve back time in meetings, or when the whole team—not just you—creates uninterrupted periods of quality time for high-value work.

And because you are making these adjustments as a team, no one is put off when their email is not answered within seconds, when the meeting is scheduled for only 20 minutes, or if you politely decline when they ask, "Got a minute?" There is a compounding effect when no one in your organization is checking email at the dinner table. Like you, they'll be enjoying their time away from the office, with their friends and family, knowing they've maximized the quantity and quality of their workday, arriving the next day rested and fresh.

Activity Is Not Progress

1. Start by creating quantity.
   a. Compress your meeting times to 20 and 40 minutes to save six hours a week.
   b. OHIO solves for task switching and the residual effect, which are cognitive realities that waste your time.
   c. Be excellent at saying "no," which can also come in the form of lowering what is being requested of you.

2. Separate your tasks into Newport's deep and shallow work categories. Understanding the difference allows you to schedule your day to take advantage of both types of work.

3. Then create quality:
   a. Create uninterrupted time.
   b. Know your chronotype.
   c. Control your environment.

4. Quantity of work and quality of work go hand in hand. By improving quality, you also expand quantity.

9 Make Your Day to Make Your Month

What is important is seldom urgent, and what is urgent is seldom important.

—Dwight D. Eisenhower

John Serino and I together ran a retail chain with more than 115 locations across five states. John was fond of telling his team, "Make your day to make your week. Make your week to make your month." He understood that success comes from stacking together hundreds of well-executed days.

But since time is not a renewable resource, doing so requires planning out each day. Not just when you feel out of control, but all of the days, without exception. The consequence of not doing so leaves you squandering vast portions of your time doing things that don't matter. Absent a plan, instead of completing the work that adds value to your organization, you'll blow time on the "shiny objects" and "dumpster fires" that draw us like a moth to the flame—which is not where you want to go if you're the moth.

There's a reason for this: it's how we're programmed, and this is the first step to changing our behavior. As humans we evolved to respond to urgent stimulus, whether it's a charging saber-tooth tiger or a foraging gazelle. The amygdala is a part of the brain that controls emotion, and for centuries, it developed to over-index on immediate events because that is what kept us alive and fed. Activities that benefit from longer term thinking, like farming or operating a business, are relatively new to the human consciousness. Dr. Neil Lewis and Dr. Daphna Oyserman described the underlying neural science, explaining, "People assume they should attend to the present; their future self can handle the future,"[1] which is a more polished way of saying that we are neurologically programmed to rush toward dumpster fires. Absent a plan, we gravitate toward whatever is urgent, regardless of its strategic or tactical importance. To offset our biology, we need to use some of the tactics developed by the former Supreme Allied Commander and by the most famous health and fitness celebrity of all time.

General Eisenhower's Matrix

During World War II, Dwight Eisenhower faced relentless tension between urgent issues and winning the war. To guide his staff, he developed what became known as the *Eisenhower matrix* (Figure 9.1):

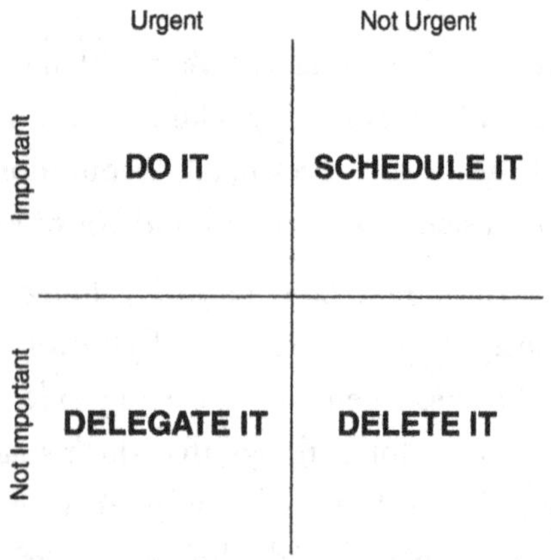

	Urgent	Not Urgent
Important	DO IT	SCHEDULE IT
Not Important	DELEGATE IT	DELETE IT

Figure 9.1 The Eisenhower Matrix

Without a plan for the whole day, our biology pulls us to the bottom row of the Eisenhower matrix. But to win a war, or run an organization, your time should be concentrated in the upper row—and ideally in the upper right quadrant. But since our nature pulls us in the other direction, we need to offset that pressure with the power of routine.

Which brings me to the fitness expert, Jack LaLanne, who did more to revolutionize everyday fitness and health than anyone before or after. But his secret power was not jumping jacks or broccoli. It was his power of routine. LaLanne ate 10 raw vegetables a day—not 9 or 11, but exactly 10. He understood that if his routine had been "eat a lot of veggies," day by day that helping of broccoli would have been reduced, perhaps even replaced, with a handful of Milk Duds. LaLanne knew that absent a routine, it was unrealistic to resist the temptations that pull us into watching TikTok or diving into a low-value staff emergency.

The same is true when it comes to implementing the Eisenhower matrix. Absent a ritual, we arrive at the office ambushed by emails, employees asking, "Got a minute?" and Slack channels blowing up. The day is spent in the lower row. You reassure yourself that the next day will be different. But of course, it isn't. You fail to make your day, which as Serino would tell you, guarantees that you won't make your month.

The Planning Ritual

Initially, I resisted structuring my day. I convinced myself that between my innate discipline and my above average smarts, those guardrails were for others. But that was arrogance and laziness. It mostly made it easier for me to do what suited me in the moment, instead of what added the most value to my stakeholders. I also thought the idea of a ritual was a bit hokey. But my days were not getting better. I had to try something new.

When I did, I came to see ritual as essential to establishing a new set of habits and practices. Which is why I want to walk you through what has become my own daily routine. Not to convince you of my particular method, but instead to illustrate an example, and show you how quick and simple a planning ritual can be.

I try to go to bed and wake up at the same time. When I wake, I make the same type of coffee, and sit in the same chair. There I read the news in the same order. I set a time limit of 25 minutes for reading the news. Then awake with the help of my coffee, I complete a short meditation. I next review my email, responding to simple messages but not allowing myself to be drawn into any projects, reading attachments, or messages that may require a detailed response.

At this point I plan the day, using a table of five columns that I created in a simple Word document (Figure 9.2). I prefer this over all the apps and other planners for sale or download that I've tried (and I've tried quite a few!).

Date	Tactical Statement	Q3 Priorities	Deep Work	Shallow Work
6/12				
6/13				

Figure 9.2 Daily Planning Tool

I begin by typing out my tactical statement (Figure 9.3). It doesn't change day to day. It is an affirmation of the methods that are required for me to meet my quarterly priorities. You'll notice that my tactical statement reflects subskills from this book, such as adhering to my priorities, or working on saying "no." I never cut and paste the words, for me it's important to type them out. I then type out my quarter's priorities. I do these two steps to remind me of what is important and where I want to focus my time *before* I list the day's tasks. It's a way to remain mindful of the Eisenhower matrix.

Date	Tactical Statement	Q3 Priorities	Deep Work	Shallow Work
6/12	Build teams wherever possible; stay focused on a narrow set of high impact objectives; seek advice where possible; be excellent at saying no.	Implement new bonus plan. Hire sales manager. Design exit interview process.		
6/13				

Figure 9.3 Daily Planning Tool

I then write down any tasks, using Newport's categorization of deep and shallow work (Figure 9.4). It's important to write these down, even the things you are certain you won't forget. There is strong evidence that trying to keep your to-do list by memory occupies a substantial portion of your attention and interferes with your creativity. Long, running to-do lists also allow you to pick and choose which tasks you want to do in the moment, leading you to overspend your time in the bottom row of the Eisenhower matrix. Writing down your to-do list also reduces stress, as once it's on the list you're certain you won't forget it, and more confident when it will be completed.

Date	Tactical Statement	Q3 Priorities	Deep Work	Shallow Work
6/12	Build teams wherever possible; stay focused on a narrow set of high impact objectives; seek advice where possible; be excellent at saying no.	Implement new bonus plan. Hire sales manager. Design exit interview process.	Review sales manager resumes. Brainstorm new sales commission plan.	Review new lease. Call plumber. Set sales manager interview schedule.
6/13			Write out interview questions for sales manager.	Cancel flight to Chicago. Determine who should be part of the interviewing team.
6/14			Prepare for call with tax CPA.	

Figure 9.4 Daily Planning Tool

Tasks I don't plan to do in that day are activated to the future, creating a series of realistic daily lists. A study on compliance of breast self-exams during a 30-day period showed that there was a 100% compliance rate for women who indicated *when* they were going to perform the exam versus 53% of those who did not. A related study asked drug addicts in treatment to perform a daily writing exercise. Eighty percent of those who scheduled when they planned to complete their writing succeeded, while those who did *not* had near zero compliance.

I next number my tasks in the order in which I plan to complete them, taking into consideration my chronotype, their urgency, and prioritizing deep work (Figure 9.5). I complete things in the determined order, which keeps me from gravitating toward low-value work, or finding excuses to push off something I don't want to do.

Date	Tactical Statement	Q3 Priorities	Deep Work	Shallow Work
6/12	Build teams wherever possible; stay focused on a narrow set of high impact objectives; seek advice where possible; be excellent at saying no.	Implement new bonus plan. Hire sales manager. Design exit interview process.	1 Review sales manager resumes. 2 Brainstorm new sales commissions plan.	5 Review new lease. 4 Call plumber. 3 Set sales manager interview schedule.
6/13			Write out interview questions for sales manager.	Cancel flight to Chicago. Determine who should be part of the interviewing team.
6/14			Prepare for call with tax CPA.	

Figure 9.5 Daily Planning Tool

I like crossing things off my list, and there's a reason. Research shows that when we put a line through the task, our brain erases the task from our active memory, freeing up capacity. It also gives us a micro-dose of dopamine as a reward, which helps improve compliance.

Saturday is my cheat day. On Saturday, I sleep as late as I can and do whatever I want, without any regard to a plan. It's my least efficient day, but having a cheat day makes it easier to maintain my routine the rest of the week.

What should be obvious by now is that my planning ritual takes less than a few minutes each morning. It does not require any special apps or tools, nor any major change to my general work conventions. But what it does do is add hours to my productivity and is vital to adhering to my priorities.

Eat the Frog First

The French writer Nicholas Chamfort wrote, "If it's your job to eat a frog, it's best to do it first thing in the morning. And if it's your job to eat two frogs, it's best to eat the biggest one first." When I put off an unpleasant task, it's a drag on my attention and creativity. Every time I consider getting to it, I negotiate with myself, make excuses to procrastinate, all the while reminded that at some point I'll have to eat that frog. I can also be quite skillful about avoiding eating the frogs, or as James Parker of *The Atlantic* writes:[2]

> *Straining to avoid one particular thing, dawdling mightily, you can do five others. You can clean the house. You can exercise. You can work on a book. The wrong book, but still—a book. If you organize yourself skillfully, you can be productive and even sort of professional while not doing what you're supposed to be doing.*

What I discovered is that I'm not only most productive, I'm also happiest, when I eat the frog as early in the day as I can. Provided it does not interfere with time spent on deep work, once the frog is gone, I'm free from thinking about it ever again. For me, I might as well just eat the frog, get the dopamine hit when I cross it off the list, and enjoy the remainder of my day.

The Power of Immersion

Jack Dorsey, the cofounder of Twitter, gives each day a theme.[3] For example, Wednesdays are for marketing and communications, Thursdays for developers and technology. He does so because there is a creativity and productivity curve that expands exponentially upward as you involve yourself in single-subject work.

There is also a compounding effect on your creative process when you focus on one problem continuously. It's because your creative mind is not like your logical or mathematical mind. Our brains work more like a web of short circuits than a single pathway. The wires cross at unexpected places, sparks jump, and these short circuits lead to critical insights. It's why one thought leads to another, as the expression goes. A prior insight is a requirement to getting to the next, as the spark jumps across neurons, which in combination creates breakthroughs. We call this "creativity," and it can only happen during spans of attention where you light up the wires in unison, enabling creative short circuits.

Creativity is fueled by your brain's ability to access prior stimulus, such as a paragraph you just read, or a partially formed idea. These memories are stored in neural networks and rely on patterns or relationships that travel along the brain's limbic system.[4] The amygdala is the switching station, and by flooding it with a single subject, like Dorsey's focus on marketing all day, we open more pathways of related information and create the short circuits that lead to creative insights and breakthroughs.

While you don't have to make your whole day monothematic, nor may that be possible, you can cluster similar-themed work into adjacent blocks of time. Returning to my plan for the day, I'll take advantage of my neurology and shift the shallow work of determining who should be on the interview team alongside the deep work of setting up the interview schedule (Figure 9.6).

Date	Tactical Statement	Q3 Priorities	Deep Work	Shallow Work
6/12	Build teams wherever possible; stay focused on a narrow set of high impact objectives; seek advice where possible; be excellent at saying no.	Implement new bonus plan. Hire sales manager. Design exit interview process.	1 Review sales manager resumes. *2 Write out interview questions for sales manager.*	5 Call plumber. 4 Set sales manager interview schedule. *3 Determine who should be part of the interviewing team.* *6 Cancel flight to Chicago.*
6/13			*Brainstorm new sales commission plans.*	*Review new lease.*
6/14			Prepare for call with tax CPA.	

Figure 9.6 Daily Planning Tool

For the same reason, even though I don't need them right away, it makes sense to write out the interview questions immediately following reviewing the candidate's resumes. Not only will it likely avoid me having to unnecessarily re-read the resumes the following day, I'll leverage the power of immersion and almost certainly create more insightful questions. Grouping the interview plan in this way increases the *quality* of my work and eliminates unnecessary task switching, saving time and creating *quantity*—such that with the extra capacity, I can move up the task of canceling the Chicago flight.

Done Is Better than Perfect

Sheryl Sandberg, the former chief operating officer of the parent company of Facebook, famously said, "Done is better than perfect." Similar to how we avoid the frogs, we are drawn to the work that we enjoy and often overstay our welcome. To illustrate Sandberg's point, imagine a curve with the *x*-axis representing time spent on the task, and the *y*-axis the final quality of the work (Figure 9.7). Eventually, the slope of the curve decreases as the extra effort provides little incremental value—or diminishing returns. But because we enjoy the work (or want to avoid what is next on the list) we keep at it, wasting our time.

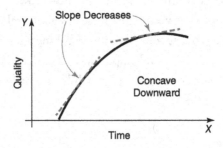

Figure 9.7 Done Versus Perfect Curve

In my own case, I enjoy writing—even an email. I often catch myself editing and making minor adjustments, attempting to perfect an email that will in the end be read by the recipient with such haste that all my Hemingway flourishes are nothing more than self-indulgences. The problem is that I'm only human. I need guardrails, which is why I often give myself a time limit for tasks that I know I enjoy.

Remember to Think

Before taking over leadership at IBM, which at the time was the world's preeminent technology company, Thomas Watson was a senior manager at a competing computer company. During an unproductive sales meeting, he became frustrated and barked, "The trouble with every one of us is that we don't *think* enough. We get paid for working with our *heads*." Then he wrote the word "THINK" on an easel in all caps. It became such a bulwark for his work-philosophy that when he eventually became head of IBM, they named the company magazine *THINK*.

I saw this in practice when I was on the board of directors of Asurion. Over time, Asurion grew to employ 23,000 people across 14 countries. A driver of that success was that Kevin Taweel, the chief executive officer, was committed to making sure he had time to *THINK*. Kevin understood the importance of not confusing activity for progress. To this day, he considers putting his feet on the desk and staring out the window a critical part of his job description.

Finding time to *THINK* can be as simple as not checking your phone messages while you're standing in line for coffee or allowing time after reading a report to reflect on what you've just read. It's about taking a pause before entering a meeting to collect your thoughts. Rushing from place to place may provide a feeling of headway and importance, but that's office theater. Your most consequential work often takes place while driving home, taking a walk, or staring out the window.

A Final Thought . . .

I don't expect you to structure your day exactly as I do. You may not type out a tactical statement or meditate in the morning. But there are universal elements that must be integrated into your workflow if you want to consistently make your day to make your month. These subskills include creating a daily plan, using ritual and routine, eating the frogs first, clustering similar projects together, creating deep work time, avoiding task switching, finding time to THINK, and remembering that done is better than perfect.

Once I did all this, I discovered an unexpected bonus. My days became deeply satisfying and more fulfilling. Put another way, it made me happier. I have more time for a life outside of work. Not just in terms of hours, but also my focus and attention. When I'm with friends at dinner I don't look at my email while they place their order. I read more books. I exercise regularly. I'm fully present when I play with my grandchildren. All the while, knowing my day was managed well, my work is complete and I'm likely to make my month.

When we misuse our time, we exchange part of our life too cheaply. Thoreau was mindful of the toll that these tasks (what he called "things") have on our soul. To him, our time is the most important thing we possess. Recklessly trading away part of our day is giving up a portion of our life—or as he writes, "The cost of a thing is the amount of what I will call life, which is required to be exchanged for it, immediately or in the long run."

Make Your Day to Make Your Month

1. Time is not a renewable resource. Plan each day without exception.

2. The amygdala, which controls emotion, evolved to over-index on immediate events (aka, shiny objects and dumpster fires).

3. Categorize tasks into Eisenhower's matrix:

	Urgent	Not Urgent
Important	DO IT	SCHEDULE IT
Not Important	DELEGATE IT	DELETE IT

4. Establishing a ritual is a requirement to consistently planning your day.

5. Every day, write down your personal tactical statement and quarterly goals.

6. Categorize tasks into shallow work and deep work.

7. Number your tasks in the order you want to do them. Consider your chronotype as you do so.

8. Time-activate your future work so you don't have to remember it, and you know it will get completed.

9. Use the power of immersion: cluster similar tasks into themes.

10. Eat the frog first.

11. Create time to THINK, which is the time you'll create the most value for your organization.

12. Remember that done is better than perfect.

10 Curing the Digital Disaster

A day can really slip by when you're deliberately avoiding what you're supposed to do.

—Bill Watterson

When most information arrived in our mailbox and not on our computer or phone, the typical executive received about 1,000 communications per year. Today that number has increased to 30,000![1] We spend a mind-numbing five hours per day processing email,[2] even though 40% of the email we receive we don't consider useful. That means every day we waste two hours alone with unnecessary email, before considering text messages, voice mail, and other collaboration platforms. What was supposed to save us time and make us more efficient has become a productivity ball and chain.

As the cost and ease of communication plummeted, it's become too easy to send a spreadsheet or a 30-page PowerPoint presentation to a dozen people. We increasingly define our productivity by our ability to respond to an inbox full of other people's demands rather than working on what we know to be important. The elite consulting firm McKinsey & Company observed in a piece they aptly named "If we're all so busy, why isn't anything getting done?" "Interacting is easier than ever, but true, productive, value-creating collaboration is not.

And what's more, where engagement is occurring, its quality is deteriorating. This wastes valuable resources, because every minute spent on a low-value interaction eats into time that could be used for important, creative, and powerful activities."[3]

For years, I viewed these intrusions as an unavoidable curse of the modern era—until I came across research at Harvard Business School that tracked 27 high-performing CEOs over three months.[4] The research team analyzed how these CEOs spent their time in 15-minute increments, 7 days a week, 24 hours a day. They eventually accumulated 60,000 hours of data. What they found is that the most effective CEOs were ruthless about not allowing email and other forms of digital communication to take over their time and attention. When I dug deeper, I found they were able to do so not by disconnecting from the modern world, but by applying a handful of very simple habits and practices.

Dopamine and Continuous Partial Attention

"Attention is the most powerful tool of the human spirit," Linda Stone, founder of the Attention Project, writes. Her research led to the identification of a concept she calls "continuous partial attention," exposing the common myth of multitasking. It begins with understanding the difference between cognitive and mechanical tasks.[5] Stirring the soup while talking on the phone is an example of multitasking. So, too, is listening to a podcast while running on the treadmill. In both cases we're able to accomplish two things in the time it would otherwise take to accomplish only one. But this is true because one of the two tasks requires cognition while the other is mechanical.

In contrast, combining two cognitive tasks, such as participating in a meeting while reading email, is behaviorally impossible. Because we have only one frontal lobe, our brains process cognitive tasks serially. Parallel processing for cognitive work is impossible. We may think we are performing two cognitive activities at the same time, but what we are actually doing is rapidly switching back and forth between the two tasks (split-second *task switching*)—which is inefficient and obstructs our concentration. Unlike stirring soup while on the phone, you can't listen while speaking, or write while doing math. It is not a skill you can learn. Your frontal lobe can only send one cognitive signal at a time.

We convince ourselves we're being more efficient, but we're toggling back and forth mostly for the dopamine. Allow me to explain. *Dopamine* is the feel-good neurotransmitter we release when our brains are expecting or receiving a reward, such as chocolate, a big sale, or sex. Dopamine also leads to alertness, focus, and motivation. It's why the drug Adderall, which raises the level of dopamine in our brain, is the drug of choice for late-night studying on college campuses. The satisfaction we get from responding to a text or even deleting junk messages also releases dopamine. We drift to our email when we feel bored or the work we're doing is unengaging. As we do so, the satisfaction we feel is not because we accomplished something useful. It's because we got a nourishing micro-dose of dopamine.

Eighty-four percent of us leave our email application always open,[6] giving ourselves a constant alternative to paying attention in the meeting, reading the mind-numbing 40-page lease, or working on that new healthcare plan. It's why we skip the hard emails and read the easy ones: deleting junk mail, clicking through to a news link, or knocking out a few email replies. Dopamine also explains why, even though we know it's rude, when we get a text message in the middle of dinner, we feel the itch to read it—even if the person across from us is in the middle of a sentence. A social connection triggers dopamine, whether it be in an email, text, or Instagram post: *Someone is connecting with me . . . and that feels good.*

Yet while the dopamine feels good in the moment, it adds little value to our organization. Sarah Peck summed this up in the *Harvard Business Review*: "Sending messages speedily makes us think we're important instead of taking time to really chew on ideas, and it punts work onto other people's agendas rather than asking us to figure things out ourselves."[7]

Gaining 80 Additional Minutes Each Day

There is no shortage of apps and software we can buy and download that offer to undo the productivity damage caused by the other productivity apps and software that we already bought and downloaded. The cure to all this comes not from buying more technology, but through simplification—that's what I observed after reading the Harvard study of the 27 high-performing CEOs. Those top performing managers had no patience for the latest tools and apps that further complicate their communication. They all employ a version of four modest reforms, that work instantly, and in my case gained me 80 minutes of additional high-quality time—every day.

Check Messages Less Often

I once hired a former US Army colonel as a regional vice president, who among other things had previously worked with a team of senior military officials to map out the invasion of Iraq. In one conversation he told me he only checks email three times a day. I found that strange given most of us open 70% of our email within six seconds of its arrival[8] and unlock our phone 80 times a day.[9] I asked him how he managed to design a complex military operation while checking his email so infrequently. He bluntly answered, "Nothing I was sent required less than three hours' response time. We had an invasion to plan."

Constantly checking our email or other collaboration tools is mostly about avoiding deep work or things we don't want to do. In so doing we pay the toll of task switching and forgo the benefits of immersion. But there are two simple steps that will materially reduce how often you check for messages, and they are about controlling your environment.

Begin by turning off notifications that alert you to incoming email, text messages, and other digital messaging. That alert is designed to be an irresistible dopamine monster roaring, "Stop whatever you're doing and read me." Instead of pretending you'll resist it through force of will, control your environment by turning off the notifications.

Further control your environment by closing out of email and collaborative applications after you've responded to the messages. Then set a time when you'll check them again. My own goal is to check email four times a day, beginning first thing in the morning, twice during the workday, and then once before I end my day. In this way, no email is left unattended for more than three hours. If this feels too much to ask, begin by checking your messages once an hour, always closing out of the applications afterward. As you respond to your messages, observe whether the outcome would have changed had you waited an additional hour. My hunch is that you'll soon realize that four times a day is plenty—after all, you have an invasion to plan.

Ruthlessly Unsubscribe

The name we use for junk email comes from a 1970 Monty Python comedy sketch, where two customers try to order off the breakfast menu in a restaurant occupied by Vikings. Everything on the menu includes Spam, even the Lobster Thermidor. In the sketch, Spam is everywhere, unavoidable, and unwanted.

For years, I didn't worry about all the electronic pork I was force-fed because it takes so little time to hit the delete button. But in writing this book I decided to track my behavior. I saw that the purveyors of spam know what they are doing. Instead of deleting, more often than I realized I took the bait—and those instances added up. The breaking news alert that I clicked through wasn't warning me of a major news event that couldn't wait, but was instead a marketing ploy to draw me away from my work to view their advertisements. Once there, they'd hold me for as long as they could with photographs, videos, other links, and related news. In my case, incoming spam diverted me to the tune of 37 minutes every day!

I suppose I should feel lucky it was just 37 minutes. In 2020, Americans spent an average of 147 minutes a day on social media, a frightening increase over the 90 minutes we spent in 2012.[10] It's because these interruptions are getting louder and more effective. This understanding matters because the most important step to curing the addiction is accepting there are economic forces that want our attention. More and more we are becoming modern-day lab rats hitting the silicon pedal to release dopamine. The social media hucksters are really good at what they do. They track our every keystroke and analyze what causes us to linger on their sites. As Josh Marshall writes in *The*

Atlantic, there is a "chronic oversupply of publications chasing a fixed number of ad dollars,"[11] which means there is an economic arms race to get us to stop our productive work to look at their ads.

We're no match for the squads of Silicon Valley geniuses who make their living finding ways to tap us on our shoulder with a digital "Got a minute?" The only option is to *control your environment.* As you eliminate the notifications from your news subscriptions, ruthlessly unsubscribe from all but the most essential email lists.

Having done so, today I read the news on my schedule. I shop when I have a need instead of when an algorithm finds something to sell me. I avoid the temptation to read the latest blog, post, or newsletter that does not represent my priorities. Altogether, ruthlessly unsubscribing gave me 37 minutes of my life back, each and every day.

Delete. Respond. Defer.

An estimated 37% of emails that require a response or action are deferred or rescheduled after being only partially read.[12] There is no better place to implement *OHIO* than with your digital communication. The *Harvard Business Review* estimates that failing to do so costs us 27 minutes every day:[13]

> *When we check a crowded inbox, we end up re-reading emails over and over again. We can't help it; if they're there, we read them . . . if people go to their inboxes 15 times per day and spend just four seconds looking at each email (the time it takes to read the average preview text) and re-reading only 10% of them (an estimate based on the number of messages that fit on average computer screen), they'll lose 27 minutes each day.*

With each email you have three—and only three—correct choices: *delete, respond,* or *defer.* Try first to delete or respond, but for those you must defer don't leave them in your inbox to nag at you at a combined cost of 27 minutes each day. Instead, activate it to a future time on your to-do list, or use an email application that defers the message, such as Boomerang, Superhuman, or FollowUpThen, to a time when you are confident you can fully respond.

Five Rules for Email Efficiency

Set a culture within your organization that makes clear you're going to efficiently use your email and collaboration tools. Insist on five simple rules:

1. Include only recipients who can act based on the information, or who are required to understand the content. The ease of adding recipients to an email is not an excuse to force others to waste time reading unactionable emails.

2. Before using "Reply All," review the list of recipients and delete the addresses of people who won't find the information useful or actionable.

3. Never send uncurated attachments unless the entire content is necessary. For example, if only a few pages of a PowerPoint presentation are relevant, send only those pages or call out which pages to read.

4. As the subject of an email string evolves to new topics, create a new email and subject heading. Long email strings, which force the reader to re-read prior emails, but save the sender a few seconds re-typing the correct list of recipients or a new subject heading, is an act of digital selfishness.

5. Don't ask the same question of multiple people when you need just one response. Digital "jump ball" makes the sender's life easy, but misuses other people's time.

These five rules of email efficiency are not controversial and can be implemented throughout your organization in less than two minutes by sending a picture of this page to your entire team.

A Final Thought . . .

Michael Mankins, Chris Brahm, and Greg Caimi, writing in the *Harvard Business Review*, note an unwanted result of low-cost communication: "As the incremental cost of one-to-one and one-to-many communications declined, the number of interactions radically multiplied . . . . If the trend is left unchecked, executives will soon be spending more than one day out of every week just managing electronic communications."[14] That time has already arrived.

This makes it critical that you leverage your *entire* organization in this effort. It is one thing for you to gain control over your own electronic communication. In a competitive world, imagine the impact you'll make if your whole organization does so as well. Efficient electronic communication can become a competitive weapon as you strive to outperform your rivals. While you oversee a high-performing team, let your competition spend a third of their work week reading news alerts, keeping up on Hollywood gossip, and glancing at texts during important meetings, while your team gets their work done, and clobbers your rivals in the marketplace.

Curing the Digital Disaster

1. It is impossible to engage in two cognitive tasks in parallel. Rapid task switching is not multitasking.

2. Do not mistake dopamine hits for productivity.

3. Restrict checking your messages to four times a day. Close out your email when you're not checking messages.

4. Eliminate alerts and ruthlessly unsubscribe from email lists.

5. With email and collaborative platforms, take one of only three actions: Delete. Respond. Defer. This is the digital version of OHIO.

6. Create a culture of effective digital communication across your whole organization. Send out to your organization the five rules for email efficiency:

   a. Include only those email recipients who need to know or can act on the information.

   b. Review the recipient list before using "Reply All."

   c. Do not send uncurated attachments.

   d. Begin new email strings as the subject matter evolves.

   e. Don't ask the same question of multiple people when you need just one response.

11 Seven Steps to Running a Great Meeting

Any man who can drive safely while kissing a pretty girl is simply not giving the kiss the attention it deserves.

—Albert Einstein

The meeting started late and went over the scheduled time. Attendees were updated on events that had already occurred. Speakers talked too long and repeated themselves in unstructured presentations. Those on video tried to surreptitiously knock off some email while trying to appear fully present. No forward-facing decisions were made. "Meetings are broken," Amy Bonsall writes in the *Harvard Business Review,* and they are only getting worse since COVID-19:[1]

> *Something happened when work moved online in 2020 and opening up the office hasn't fixed it. Every interaction with colleagues became a video call, and our days became a game of transactional Tetris: Where can I slot in this or that meeting? [and] the Tetris has gotten more complex.*

In a survey conducted by the consulting firm Bain & Company,[2] executives spent 23 hours a week in meetings, and more than 50% of those meetings were viewed as "ineffective" or "very ineffective."[3] Even before the pandemic, things were worsening, as meeting time had increased by more than 10 hours per week.[4] This is because shared calendars and scheduling tools make it easier to create a meeting and include a larger list of attendees. Today's ubiquitous use of video conferencing and cell phones means we now have few logistical constraints to convening a meeting.

It does not have to be this way. Leaders, such as Sheryl Sandberg and Jeff Bezos, are obsessive about when and how to assemble their teams, and there are seven easy steps, which taken together, are guaranteed to compress your meeting time and make them significantly more productive.

1. Require a Purpose

Most meetings are nothing more than updates on what has happened in the past, while only a sliver of the time is spent on how to make better forward-facing decisions (Figure 11.1).

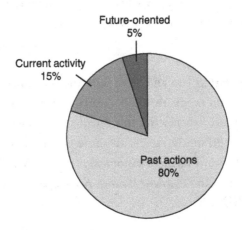

Figure 11.1 Time in Meetings

The easy solution is to have every meeting begin by answering this question: "What is the problem we're trying to solve, or the opportunity we're trying to capture, and how can each of us help?" If organizers don't have an answer to the question, they're likely signing up valuable people for a wasted hour. Let's look at an example of the power of this simple question:

> *The purpose today is to solve the delays in getting shipments out on time. We want to leave this meeting with a plan that improves on-time shipment by 17% and a list of who does what.*

This statement concentrates the meeting on a specific *purpose*. The meeting organizer now knows to present background information and discuss historical results only to the extent that it helps address the question. By sharpening the purpose, they'll drive the meeting toward forward-facing actions and not allow the conversation to meander as people tell stories, repeat themselves, or offer unnecessary information. This narrowing of focus will help turn that one-hour meeting into 40 high-impact minutes.

As you present background information, and discuss historical results, consider how best to convey that information. Quite often presenting background material in a meeting is slower and less robust than alternatives such as a pre-meeting memo. Instead of taking the time to organize such a memo, the presenter arrives partially prepared and as a result takes too long to convey the background information. Netflix addressed this by requiring that all material be presented in advance and in a memo format, so that the time together was not spent listening to a presentation but instead in conversation and problem solving. The early data showed that by doing so, the number of meetings was reduced by an amazing 65%.[5]

2. Choose Your Attendees Intentionally

The ease with which we can add attendees, especially with mobile and video technology, has eaten into our productivity. Organizers add attendees with a few keystrokes, forgetting that by doing so they are spending the organization's dearest resource. Organizers often invite as many people as they can think to involve, instead of asking, *How can I successfully achieve the purpose with the fewest people involved?*

Not asking this question not only misuses resources, ironically it also has the impact of reducing the effectiveness of the meeting. There is often a degradation in decision-making quality as the number of people expand. Consider also that not every attendee needs to attend the entire meeting. Adjust the agenda to allow people to participate only during the relevant moments, and excuse them from the remaining topics.

Google cofounder Larry Page requires that everyone who attends a meeting actively participates. It's a sure-fire way to eliminate unnecessary attendees. I had a student challenge me on this, suggesting that adding attendees as observers helps develop long-term talent and creates inclusion. But if the goal is training and development, make that purposeful by encouraging or requiring their opinions and participation, and then spending time afterward discussing what they learned. Holding team members hostage in unnecessary meetings, where they sit in silence, causes frustration and creates a culture that is the antithesis of action.

3. Prepare a Background Memo in Advance

Similar to Netflix, while running Amazon Jeff Bezos required that each meeting begin with a short *background memo* written by the organizer. Such a memo should be concise, efficiently defining the purpose of the meeting and providing just the information necessary to meet that purpose. Requiring a memo compresses the meeting time and sharpens the presentation so that the group arrives briefed on the background information and ready to focus on a collective purpose.

As you do so, avoid formats such as PowerPoint that put graphic skills over content, often resulting in pages of unrelated bullet points and diagrams that are pointlessly complex and hard to read. Force the organizer to resist any effort to impress the attendees by showing off how much data can be compiled. Avoid raw data, and have them present only what is necessary to advance the meeting's purpose—showing their mastery of the subject by demonstrating how *little* data are required to achieve the meeting objective, not how *much* data they can present.

4. Choose a Moderator

When faced with evidence that Soviet missiles were being installed in Cuba, President John F. Kennedy convened a meeting of military aides, cabinet members, and other government officials. He understood that if he ran the meetings, people would defer to him. To generate the best decision-making, he structured these meetings to have all the members participate equally.[6] It didn't matter how many stars on their lapel. Kennedy did not want anyone deferring out of a sense of protocol, and so chose someone else as the moderator.

The moderator is the individual responsible for the process, but not necessarily the ultimate decision. The two can be separated, and you'll often find that not having the most senior person moderate the meeting creates higher-quality problem solving. A further benefit of not running every meeting yourself is that you will need to guide and train your leadership team if you want to build a substantial organization. If you pass the moderator role to others at times, and observe how effectively they run their own meetings, you can coach and develop their own meeting skills.

Moderating a meeting is a skill, and your job as a leader is to teach and develop those skills. The best moderators, for example, know to maintain an aggressive pace while not dampening participation. Long-winded participants consume everyone's time and sap the energy of the room. The moderator needs the mettle to say, "I think you've done a good job making that point. Unless there's something in addition you'd like to add, let's move to Robin." If relevant thoughts are offered out of order, the moderator can preserve the comment by using a "parking lot" to hold those ideas until later.

Skillful moderators draw out those participants less willing to speak or who present contrary points of view. This can be as simple as calling on people who are less outspoken or referring to an earlier point made by someone such as, "Sanjiv, that last observation sounds contrary to a point you made earlier, which I thought was quite interesting. How would you solve for . . . ?"

Along the way, you need to make sure that the moderator prioritizes good decision-making over social courtesies. You have an organization to run. This means a willingness to challenge ideas and push the group. Just like an athletic team doesn't win games without pushing one another, so too in organizational decision-making. As Bezos writes:

> Leaders are obligated to respectfully challenge decisions when they disagree, even when doing so is uncomfortable or exhausting. Leaders have conviction and are tenacious. They do not compromise for the sake of social cohesion.[7]

In the same vein, the moderator needs to know when to end the meeting—and the answer is not when the scheduled time is up. The reward of running a productive meeting is not to fill up the remaining minutes by adding new and unstructured topics, but to allow folks to leave the meeting early. Facebook's Sheryl Sandberg begins every meeting by reminding the team of the purpose of the meeting, which she writes on a whiteboard. As the goals are accomplished, she crosses them off. When everything is crossed off, the meeting is over.

5. Clarifying Questions

Prior to any discussion, there needs to be agreement on the facts. Former US Senator Daniel Moynihan famously said: "Everyone is entitled to [their] own opinion, but not [their] own facts."[8] Begin the meeting with *clarifying questions*. So that no one feels the need to interrupt someone else's set of questions, go around the room calling on people. In this way everyone has a chance to ask their clarifying questions.

This is not the time to dive into ideas, creativity, or recommendations but only to clarify anything in the background memo. In service to this, the moderator must control the conversation, making sure comments do not shift into opinions or discussion. While your team gets used to this step, the moderator will need to rein in those who are eager to offer their opinions, creativity, and suggestions before all clarifying questions have been asked:

> Kihan, let's first finish the clarifying questions before we get into the discussion. I've jotted down your comment, and I'll come to this first after we complete all the clarifying questions.

6. Move to Thoughts and Opinions

Now that the team understands the purpose of the meeting and has had a chance to clear up any clarifying questions, the group is in an excellent position to make effective future-oriented decisions. In doing so, the moderator can open up the meeting to an unstructured conversation or allow each person to express their opinion as called upon. The most common method is to allow everyone the freedom to talk as they choose. However, it can lead to an imbalance in the presentation of ideas, as those more senior—or more confident—speak disproportionately and make it less likely that all good ideas and challenges are aired.

To increase the chances of hearing divergent thoughts, the moderator may also choose to call on people in reverse order of seniority (as we generally do in our meetings). This reduces the opportunity for people to parrot what they think the boss wants to hear or agree with the decision that they think the boss is about to make.

The writer Chuck Palahniuk has said that listening is not waiting for your turn to talk. But in a meeting format where multiple people fight for airtime, it's hard to avoid this. Which is why having a process where the participants know that the moderator will invite everyone into the discussion before shifting topics allows the attendees to be fully present while others speak, and not channeling some attention to finding an on-ramp to enter the discussion. In so doing, prior to switching topics, have the moderator poll the group to ensure that everyone had the chance to offer their thoughts, a practice that will ease the pressure to look for these on-ramps and increase the level of attention to the points expressed by others.

7. Summarize the Meeting

The moderator must steer the conversation to a resolution of the meeting's stated purpose. Which means that before moving to another topic or ending the meeting, they should summarize what they believe the group has decided, and then ask for confirmation of that summary from everyone. This step takes only a few seconds but is critical for success.

After the meeting, the organizer should follow up with a brief written summary, generally in the form of an email or short memo. Alfred Sloan was one of the most influential leaders of General Motors and would produce a memo using a simple format:[9]

- What was decided?
- What action items are to be taken?
- Who are the parties responsible for those actions?
- What are the dates for completion?

The memo is not a summary of the meeting—no one has time to read a recitation of who said what. What matters are the answers to these four simple questions. Do so in writing. It eliminates most misunderstandings, creates a culture where an action plan comes out of every meeting, and summarizes the forward-facing information in a handful of critical sentences.

A Final Thought . . .

Establishing norms for conducting meetings requires cooperation from your entire organization. But while almost everyone agrees that meetings are broken, adding structure to the meetings is often resisted.

Challenge this. Poorly run meetings result from lazy preparation. The stakes are too high to tinker at the edges of a flawed process. Get agreement that your current meeting process is broken, then require that everyone apply the seven concepts of this chapter for a 100-day trial period. Don't debate the steps; just accept what you are doing is broken and make these steps your new baseline.

Along the way, the team may try to regress to those old, frustrating, habits. Fight the temptation. Your team needs to witness the benefits of the seven steps before they know where to make changes. After 100 days, debrief with your team and decide what, if anything, to modify. Then build and enforce your final meeting design principles into your daily work habits.

Seven Steps to Running a Great Meeting

1. Define the purpose of the meeting. "What is the problem you're trying to solve, or opportunity you're trying to capture, and how can each attendee help?"

2. Choose your attendees intentionally. "How can I successfully achieve the purpose with the *fewest* people involved?"

3. Prepare a brief background memo. Focus on substance over style. Include only the data that is relevant to the meeting purpose.

4. Choose a moderator. They are responsible for the process, but not necessarily the decision.

5. Establish a single set of facts. Use the background memo and clarifying questions to make sure everyone understands the situation.

6. Then move to thoughts and opinions. Manage the conversation so everyone participates. Consider involving people in reverse order of seniority.

7. Summarize the action items, verbally at the end of each topic and in a short written summary immediately following the meeting. Use this format:

   What was decided?

   What action items are to be taken?

   Who are the parties responsible for those actions?

   What are the dates for completion?

12 Delegating

The really expert riders of horses let the horse know immediately who is in control, but then guide the horse with loose reins and seldom use the spurs.

—Sandra Day O'Connor, former Supreme Court justice

I n the developing world, dirt floors are a major source of disease. Pathogens survive in the soil, and dust is a principal cause of respiratory disease. Gayatri Datar was determined to change this. By experimenting with the mud from a dried-out lake near Stanford, she and a team of classmates discovered a coating process that seals an earthen floor for a fraction of the price of concrete. She was on her way to changing the lives of a billion people.

Gayatri moved to Rwanda and started EarthEnable, a social enterprise that installs healthy and affordable floors. For two years she made progress by working as many hours as she could. Mistaking delegation for lightening her own workload, she passed along some of her work to others, but when something was not done to her satisfaction, she'd often take it back and do it herself.

Unsurprisingly, EarthEnable's growth stalled. They missed their targets because her management methods were not scalable. There was only one Gayatri, and if EarthEnable had any hope of reaching millions of vulnerable families, she needed to fundamentally change her leadership style. Calling me from her home in Rwanda, she said:

> *At first, I was the driver. I was the mason scheduler. I was the varnish maker and installer. I built all aspects of the business, and it was super fun. Now I see that growing a business means you stop producing output and shift energy to building an organization.*

Managing Managers

Many emerging leaders, as they face a growing to-do list, resort to working harder and longer hours as a way to scale. But managing is different than doing, and increasing your personal velocity doesn't scale as your organization expands, especially as you make the leap to managing managers. Let me explain.

Most of us begin our careers as individual contributors. Our success is measured almost exclusively by what we alone produce—a great presentation, for example, or closing a sale. Our value is measured by our individual wit and effort and to some extent how many hours we're willing to work.

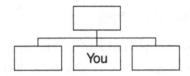

Even when managing a single department or a small team, throwing more hours against the challenge often works. For example, if one of your direct reports prepares a presentation that you're not happy with, you can stay late at the office and rewrite the presentation.

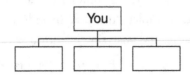

But working harder isn't scalable once you begin to manage managers.

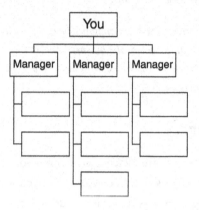

At this point it is impossible to cover for the deficiencies of others. Furthermore, even if you had the capacity, you can't routinely bypass managers who work for you, and complete the work of one of their direct reports. There is only one solution if you want to build a lasting organization—you must learn the craft of delegation.

Skills, Capacity, and Capability

What changed everything for EarthEnable was largely a matter of Gayatri learning how to delegate. She had a great product. She just needed to figure out how to scale her organization. Gayatri began to realize that delegation was not handing off errands to someone else, but instead it was expanding capability within her organization.

Delegation begins by first separating the *task* in front of you from the *skills* required to accomplish that task. For instance, imagine you need to create a staffing plan for a one-time summer sale at your toy store. That is a task. But the skills to complete the task include creating a spreadsheet, reviewing past foot traffic, and analyzing historical sales to make forecasts.

No doubt you can get the staffing plan done faster if you miss dinner with your family and do it yourself. But you will have sacrificed the chance to build skills and capability within your organization that will carry into other tasks, such as the holiday schedule, the annual operating plan, the decision whether to stay open later on Sundays, and eventually staffing for a dozen toy stores instead of just one—none of which you need in order to complete the staffing plan for the summer sale.

Because delegating a new skill often takes longer than doing it yourself, in deciding whether the organization will get sufficient payback for that investment estimate how many times, and how many hours, you spend applying that skill over a six-month span. If it's 10 hours, the *six-month rule* suggests you would be willing to spend 10 extra hours teaching that skill to someone else rather than continuing to do it yourself.

Delegating is also a tool in evaluating a team member's *capability*. If you are deciding whether to promote your leading salesperson to sales manager, delegation can be a tool in determining if the person is up for the promotion. In a case we teach at Stanford, Melanie Dulbecco, the CEO of the food manufacturing company Torani, maker of syrups and flavors that are found in beverages around the world, was looking to promote someone from her sales organization to a vice president position.[1] Melanie describes to the class that by using delegation, she assigned several projects to the internal candidates and was able to quickly determine through that process who was most ready for the promotion.

Using "SCS"

SCS stands for *specific*, *co-create*, and *support* and is a mindset that captures three parallel elements of skillful delegation. By keeping SCS top of mind, you'll avoid the primary pitfalls of poor delegation. Best of all, SCS applies whether you are delegating responsibility for tomorrow's dinner reservation or the development and construction of a 200,000 square foot distribution center.

SCS: Specific

We are notoriously bad at trading hours in the future to save minutes in the present. When delegating a task, we cut corners on the upfront work of carefully defining the deliverable, saving a few moments in the present, only to chew up hours of extra time later when the work-product is not as we envisioned.

For instance, imagine you aren't sure whether to renew your office lease or search for a new location. An ineffective approach would be to ask someone, "Can you look into this and tell me whether we should renew the lease?" You may justify the expedient method by telling yourself that you're empowering the other person by leaving the details to them, but really, you're cutting corners. The end result is that you'll have wasted both your time and your employee's, as you send them back multiple times with incremental information requests, and as they waste time exploring areas that aren't a concern of yours. Alternatively, you might tell them:

Our lease is due in five months. I'm comfortable that we're paying a market price, but I'm interested in other options. See what is available and under what terms. Start with Curtis Brothers, a broker we've used before. We'll need to project square footage, by type (office, warehouse, vehicle storage), and drivetimes to our key customer locations in 20-minute geo-fences, which you can do with Geotech's mapping software. Include photos of possible locations along with key lease terms. I'm envisioning a 10-page report. I'm the only audience. Nail the content, but it does not need to be presentation quality. I'll follow this up in a short email.

The example makes it clear where you don't want them to spend time, such as reviewing the existing lease. It describes specific areas to address such as square footage requirements, and you've defined the level of quality required for the final report. You also plan to follow up these instructions with a short email, as people forget what was said. Reducing it to writing forces a level of specificity that is easy to avoid when you are delegating verbally.

This is not micromanagement. *Specificity* doesn't remove employees' freedom to apply their judgment in making their recommendations. Micromanagers are drawn into trivia that is not material to the outcome and focus on how to do things *their* way, regardless of whether it impacts the final work product. Micromanagers can't look past petty details that may not line up with how they would have performed the task. They want the charts created a certain way, using their choice of colors and font. Micromanagers expect the other person to perform as an extension of themselves. But in our example, most of the report is left open for the other person to define—and most important of all it is up to them to develop a final recommendation.

SCS: Co-Create

But what we have so far is still not ideal. So far, there's little in the way of co-creation. The wisdom of the group is almost always better than that of any one individual, so with that in mind consider the previous wording:

> . . . and [develop] drivetimes to our key customer locations in 20-minute geo-fences, which you can do with Geotech's mapping software.

Using co-create, you might consider this rewording:

> The locations of our key customer will probably be a factor in your recommendation. How do you think we should look into that?

This may, on the surface, seem like you're playing a game. After all, you know Geotech's software will do the trick. Why not just tell them what you want? The answer is that you don't hold a monopoly on creativity and imagination. They might suggest using software that takes into consideration the frequency of deliveries or to give more weight to those customers you visit more often—something you hadn't thought of.

Where you do offer specific direction, make it clear whether they can offer improvements to the plan. Because you have made it clear you want their co-creation, they might make the following helpful suggestions:

> For promising properties, how about if I just include the cut sheets already prepared by the brokers? It'll be more information than what you asked for, but will save us hours preparing custom descriptions. As well, I'd like to check with the current landlord and see if any of the adjacent space might come available in the next three years.

SCS: Support

I discovered the importance of support the hard way. A company I once ran as CEO was doubling revenue every six months. Because it was changing so fast, the senior team was tasked with work that none of us had prior experience doing. Over time, one of the managers found herself in a deeper and deeper hole. When I discovered how deep, I asked her to leave the company. But most of the fault in that situation was in how I managed my delegation.

The Russian proverb "Доверяй, но проверяй" ("trust, but verify") was popularized by Ronald Reagan during his negotiations with Soviet leader Mikhail Gorbachev, yet can be a powerful reminder for effective delegation. In providing support, set strategic checkpoints along the way instead of waiting until the end to find out if the person succeeded. Your job as a delegator is not to stand in judgment over the final work-product, nor is it to toss projects to subordinates and hope for the best, but to help your team succeed. Regular checkpoints are there to identify whether people are struggling, discover if your original plan was unclear, or identify if they need additional guidance or resources. With these checkpoints, you can make midcourse corrections that increase the chances of success.

Bring In IPF

In Chapter 3 (Instant Performance Feedback), I introduced a simple framework for providing feedback. A modification of this same framework applies in delegation (Figure 12.1).

Expectation → Measurement → Feedback →
Obstacles → Support → Alignment

Figure 12.1 Framework for Feedback

Rather than delegate in a sometimes rambling and hard-to-follow explanation, it becomes second nature for me to take the subject matter I'm delegating and describe it quickly, clearly, and efficiently using this framework.

Yours, Mine, Ours

I once hired an experienced executive and gave him the title of president while I remained the CEO. We each had our own set of direct reports, but since he reported to me, the whole company ultimately reported to me. Of course we didn't always agree on the right approach to every problem or opportunity, and that was part of the benefit of the relationship, but we knew ultimately decisions had to be made.

The problem was that I was new at having a senior partner, and tentative about exercising my authority with him. Also, I was not always clear in my decisions, which led to tense moments when one of us felt the other was reaching into their "lane." The problem was less about the underlying decision and more about the confusion about our respective roles. We hadn't developed a way to talk openly and easily about lines of authority and how decisions were to be made. The organization suffered as a result, and we had some unnecessarily tense moments between us.

It would be years before I once again promoted someone to the position of president while I again served as CEO. This time I was running an organization that operated in seven countries across multiple time zones. I had learned from my earlier experience. In this case she and I adopted the everyday phraseology of *yours, mine,* or *ours* to clarify our respective responsibilities. As decisions arose where our respective roles were not obvious, one of us would quickly check in with the other, asking if the matter in consideration was a *yours, mine,* or *ours.*

For example, in discussing whether to expand into a new country, I might tell her that the decision was an *ours*—we're making the decision together. In hiring someone reporting to her, she might say, "I'd like your advice, but ultimately I view this as a *mine.*" We didn't always agree on which it was, but unlike my prior experience, we had a simple language that left no ambiguity and was without drama or emotion. When we disagreed, we resolved the question immediately and directly with a culture of radical candor. What mattered most was that we'd clearly defined our respective lanes. The relationship was more effective because nothing went unsaid and decision-making authority was always clear.

A Final Thought . . .

John C. Maxwell, the bestselling author of *The 21 Irrefutable Laws of Leadership*, writes: "If you want to do a few small things right, do them yourself. If you want to do great things and make an impact, learn to delegate." Gayatri's innovation was of little value unless she could build an organization. Three years following our phone call, her organization quintupled in reach.

And because delegation is scalable, EarthEnable continues to accelerate its growth. Gayatri recently told me, "The sense of accomplishment I now feel, as I watch EarthEnable reach tens of thousands of families, far exceeds the minor sense of satisfaction I once had building a floor myself."

We are all conditioned by our initial experiences. Beginning as early as grade school, our successes mostly came from our individual performance. In college we were largely measured by our grades, and then in our early jobs our accomplishments mostly were in the form of reports, presentations, and analysis. Along the way, we often got further by just working harder.

None of that has much to do with being an outstanding leader. To lead well most of us have to unlearn decades of habits and practices, much like Gayatri described at the beginning of this chapter. Initially, it will not come naturally. But in learning to delegate well, if you understand the need to let go of old habits, you'll resist the pull to doing what once made you successful, and transition to the scalable form of leadership that Maxwell describes.

Delegating

1. Delegation is not about giving someone else your errands to increase your quantity of time. It is about creating skills and capacity across your organization.

2. Use delegation to evaluate talent.

3. Define the task in terms of the skills required, and look for opportunities to build those skills.

4. In deciding whether to delegate or to do it yourself, apply the *six-month rule*.

5. Delegate using SCS: specific, co-create, and support.

6. Follow up all delegation in writing, often in a short email.

7. *Trust but verify*. Support your team's success by setting up checkpoints along the way to help them succeed.

8. Develop a way to talk openly and easily about lines of authority, and how decisions are to be made using *yours*, *mine*, or *ours*.

PART III
Willingness to Seek and Take Advice

13 Five Questions

If you chase two rabbits, you will not catch either one.

—Russian proverb

A few years ago, I was in a meeting seated next to Joe Deitch where I learned an important lesson about listening. Joe started Commonwealth Financial Network; with more than $250 billion of assets under management, it is the largest privately owned, independent registered investment advisory and broker-dealer in the country. He's also the founder of the Elevate Prize, which provides critical training and resources to some of the world's most promising social entrepreneurs. In the meeting, someone made a controversial comment about a political subject. Most of us found the comment ludicrous; some openly challenged the person.

Afterward, while Joe and I were waiting for our cars, I asked him what he thought of the comment. In a soft, philosophical tone, he said, "I found it fascinating." He clarified that he wasn't persuaded by the person's views. But since there was no chance he'd change their position, he was only interested in understanding why that person held that view, as well as why others reacted so strongly. *I found it fascinating* was the consequence of Joe's perpetual sense of curiosity, and his reluctance to spend energy unnecessarily persuading others of his views.

Listen like Joe is the first essential step to seeking and taking advice. Just like many of us are with our political opinions, we waste energy trying to convince people of our own position, and generally over-index on information that confirms our prior views. Our information sources are slanted. We discount much of what does not align with our views. For these reasons, listening with curiosity is very hard, which means most people do it poorly, yet it differentiates the average manager from the highly effective manager.

Begin with Your Team

There is significant know-how and wisdom within your team, but what you learned thus far has likely been sifted through a filter, generating positions that confirm your existing views. (To repeat the quote from John Steinbeck, "No one wants advice, only corroboration.") To break away from these natural biases, you'll need to employ a structure to your fact finding.

Begin by making clear to the person you're talking with your goal and intention. They know that you need to make decisions on the direction of the organization, and to do so wisely you need their input. But if you're not clear why you're asking them for their opinions, it may leave them wondering if you are evaluating them instead, which will impact their level of openness. As a result, begin by framing the conversation in this way:

> *Like you, I care about this company. If we're going to win, I need to understand our organization not just through my own lens. I need the perspective of team members like you who see things I never see, and know more about your area of responsibility than anyone. Give me the benefit of your experience and creativity. I need your help.*

Speak to frontline employees, especially those who have day-to-day contact with your customers. You may learn more about your competitive situation, and the markets you compete in, from a customer service representative or a warehouse employee than from the vice president of this-or-that.

Now, with pen and paper in hand ask them these five questions:

- What is going well?
- What are we working on that is a waste of time?
- What do our customers care the most about?

- What are we better at than all our competitors?

- If you were me, what would you be working on?

As you collect their responses, you'll have to push them to make specific suggestions and observations. For example, "improve our quality" has limited value when compared to "our product needs to be eight pounds lighter." As you do this, you might find that some of their aspirations will seem unrealistic. But before you reject their idea, be open to the possibility that you may be held back by your own limiting beliefs or by a commitment to the status quo.

As you note their observations and ideas, avoid making promises or commitments. What you do and say will be amplified and reinterpreted, which is why you need to be cautious about setting expectations. For instance, "That's an interesting idea. I'm excited to dive in more and understand this better" avoids the impression that your *interest* in their idea is the same as agreement.

Next, Your Customers and Clients

I have witnessed many instances of managers speculating over what they thought their customers wanted, without recognizing that all they needed to do was to just ask. Your customers know why they buy (or do not buy) your product or service. They also probably know your competitors' strengths and weaknesses better than you do. And they'll likely tell you all this because it's in their best interest.

As you do so, favor depth over quantity. It may be tempting to send out a survey in an email blast, asking for numeric ratings or for them to select options from a pull-down menu. But in searching for a set of critical insights and creative ideas, you'll learn more by having a series of in-depth conversations than a thousand survey responses. Organize the conversation around five questions:

- Why do you buy from us?

- Do you buy exclusively from us or from others . . . and why?

- What are examples of things some of our competitors do better than us?

- What would we need to do to earn more of your business?
- What feature, service, or product do you wish we offered?

Don't ask these questions of only your largest customers. They come with a statistical bias as they are already satisfied with your service (that's why they are your larger customers). Speak with those who do a small amount of business with you and those that do none at all to find out why you're *not* meeting their needs and what you can do to get them to become a large customer.

If your product or service reaches hundreds, or thousands, of end users, you may need to employ outside resources to speak to enough people. But before using an outside resource, first have enough of these conversations with your customers yourself. In so doing, you'll be able to guide and train those resources on what to ask, how to ask it, and how best to react to common responses.

Then Suppliers and Vendors

After becoming a first-time CEO, I met with one of our key suppliers who flew to Dallas to meet with me. His purpose was to secure the relationship and keep our business. But what I came to appreciate in that meeting was that his company had long development and manufacturing lead times, and as a result had unique insights into the market that we did not. During my time as CEO, I came to view him as a thought partner, not as someone to squeeze for the lowest price. Which is why you should make a point to spend time with key suppliers and vendors, and ask five questions:

- Where do you see the market expanding and contracting?
- What do you think our customers value most?
- What innovations or technological changes do you see happening?
- Among our competitors, who is the best and why?
- What are examples of things that we do better than our competition?

Most of your competitor's focus will be beating them up on price. Which means you'll have a leg up on your rivals as they fail to take advantage of this fountain of information. If you play nice and take the time to build a relationship, you will likely be surprised at what they will tell you.

Last, the Competition

I was in a board meeting with a software CEO who said that whenever his company interviews current or former employees of his competitors, he makes a point of attending the interview. He wants to know more about his competition than their own CEOs do. You don't need to get into the vicinity of confidential information or trade secrets to learn a great deal about the companies who want to take away your customers. There's a mountain of legally available information that is in plain sight if you just ask.

Whether it's a casual conversation at a trade show, a job interview, or just contacting a recently departed employee and asking them to lunch, it's surprising how much information you can mine from former (and sometimes current) employees by asking five questions:[1]

- When you were there, what do you think they did well?
- What were their big challenges?
- Which competitors do they fear the most, and why?
- Why do people like to work there?
- When they lose people, what are the reasons?

Former employees are not the only way to learn from your competition. There are few secrets on the internet. Some tools can collect a startling amount of data for virtually no cost, giving you a treasure trove of information about your competitors' backlinks, traffic volume, landing pages, what phrases and words they own, and any organic keywords.

On their websites and their social media links, review job listings to see where they are expanding and in what functional areas. Once a quarter, visit job sites such as Glass Ceiling to see what is being said about them by current and former employees. Set up alerts in your search engine so you never miss anything they publish or that is said about them, and once a quarter review their websites.

Experience their lead-nurturing process by submitting questions and observing the quality and content of their responses. To help diagnose their online strategy, turn off your ad blocker, and after visiting their site, see what pops up in your own feeds. If online marketing is important to your business, track the performance of your own website against that of your competition.

A Final Thought . . .

In their 1982 book, *In Search of Excellence,* Tom Peters and Robert Waterman popularized the phrase: *management by walking around.* The theory was that if managers wandered around, spontaneously chatting with employees they happened by, they would learn important information. Their book became a business bible of sorts and sold almost a million copies each year during the first four years. The notion that wandering around was good management remained gospel for nearly four decades. But today we know that "management by walking around" is of little value in itself. Your employees are unlikely to stop you in the hallway and volunteer critical thinking. As a leader, you must have a process, structure, and purpose to all that "walking around."

For instance, the US Central Command, part of the Department of Defense, recently did just that. They understood that generals wandering the barracks was not enough. Conditioned to respect rank and authority, lower-ranking personnel were never going to impose their ideas and creativity by tapping their senior officer on the shoulder and asking, "Got a minute?" Yet the Central Command understood the value of capturing the information. "The people closest to the problems are the ones seeing and feeling the pain points firsthand," Brigadier General John Cogbill explained to the *Wall Street Journal.*[2] Which is why the Central Command set up a "Shark Tank" contest to encourage ideas to flow from the bottom up—their version of the "five questions"—to institutionalize the flow of information upward. To get the information they needed, they had to support that mission with a process and purpose.

Five Questions to Ask Employees, Customers, Suppliers, and Competitors

1. Listen with curiosity, not with an intention to confirm your existing beliefs or persuade others.

2. Ask your employees five questions. Let them know why you are asking them. Include frontline team members:
   a. What is going well?
   b. What are we working on that is a waste of time?
   c. What do our customers care the most about?
   d. What are we better at than all our competitors?
   e. If you were me, what would you be working on?

3. Ask your customers five questions. Avoid survey forms and favor depth over quantity. Be sure to ask people who *don't* do business with you:
   a. Why do you buy from us?
   b. Do you buy exclusively from us or from others . . . and why?
   c. What are examples of things some of our competitors do better than us?
   d. What would we need to do to earn more of your business?
   e. What feature, service, or product do you wish we offered?

4. Ask your suppliers five questions. They are more than a source of cheap products and services:
   a. Where do you see the market expanding and contracting?
   b. What do you think our customers value most?
   c. What innovations or technological changes do you see happening?
   d. Among our competitors, who is the best and why?
   e. What are examples of things that we do better than our competition?

5. Ask employees from the competition five questions. You'll be surprised what people will tell you:
   a. When you were there, what do you think they did well?
   b. What were their big challenges?
   c. Which competitors do they fear the most, and why?

    d. Why do people like to work there?

    e. When they lose people, what are the reasons?

6. There are no secrets on the internet. Study your competitor's online information.

7. Management by walking around is just for show. Be intentional and purposeful as you seek to learn from your employees.

14 Finding and Using Mentors

A mentor is someone who allows you to see the hope inside yourself.

—Oprah Winfrey

When I was an early investor and on the board of Asurion, which grew to several billion dollars in revenue, I watched how its CEO, Kevin Taweel, used his network of mentors as a key factor in his company's success. "The number one reason for where we are today," he later told me, "is that I surrounded the company with great advisors, and then we used them voraciously." As a business leader, you'll face very few unique problems. Generally, the answer, or a framework to find the answer, already exists. While less secure managers want to solve everything themselves, the most confident leaders know better. Sir Richard Branson, founder of the Virgin Group, underscores Kevin's experience when Branson wrote, "If you ask any successful businessperson, they will always have had a great mentor at some point along the road."

Mary Barra, the chief executive officer of General Motors, points out that the best leaders create a network of advisors. "Some executives credit one or two key people for coaching them to success, but I believe effective mentoring takes a network."[1] Mentors and advisors come from different perspectives, and the best managers seek and take advice from multiple sources, then reconcile differences—and note commonalities—before choosing the best path forward. Creating this network, though, does not come organically. To build the type of network like those of the best managers, you'll need to begin by creating a scorecard.

A Scorecard for Mentors and Advisors

Some people mistakenly believe that the best mentors come in the form of larger-than-life heroes, capable of the business equivalent of x-ray vision. They try to create relationships with famous people and their notable resumes. But just like hiring well requires a scorecard to focus on *outcomes* and *attributes*, so too does building a network of advisors. While the desired outcomes will be particular to you, there are two universal attributes of an effective advisor: *objectivity* and *pattern recognition*.

Objectivity

Objectivity is best defined as a faithfulness to the facts, coupled with self-awareness of the personal biases that come with one's view. These two characteristics are inextricably connected. As our mind processes a problem, our thought process is never free from emotional prejudice. That prejudice may lead to exaggerated optimism, unnecessary fear, or decision paralysis—while diminishing the precision of our decision-making. This bias causes us to drift from where the facts would otherwise take us. Stanford's Department of Philosophy observes, "Humans experience the world from a perspective. The contents of [individual] experiences vary greatly with [their] perspective, which is affected by [their] personal situation, and the details of [their] perceptual apparatus, language, and culture."[2]

The advantage of seeking advice is that outside advisors generally arrive with less emotional bias than the people solving their own problems. This is not to say advisors are *without* bias; they just have *less* of it. And that lessening of bias, all by itself, is a benefit of seeking and taking advice.

But you can do better than just having less bias. As you build out your team of advisors, look for and chase down those people who have a high degree of objectivity through a self awareness of what prejudice they do have.

Observe how they respond to your questions. Superstar mentors are reflective enough to begin a sentence with, "I once had a very negative experience with litigation, which impacts what I am about to say . . . ," while a person less aware of their bias might begin, "Here is what you need to understand about litigation . . . ."

It is objectivity, not a superhuman ability to problem-solve, that allows your mentors and advisors to evaluate data with greater fidelity and speed. As you identify potential advisors and cultivate your network, be alert to a person's objectivity as a key attribute of a powerful mentor.

Pattern Recognition

Pattern recognition occurs when we are faced with a situation that triggers a set of experiences accessed from our long-term memory. As we observe similar events, and the success or failure of various approaches to those events, we store most of that information. Later, our mind searches our mental hard drive for similar encounters we've had in the past. This background processing takes place primarily without our direct awareness and is the model for what is now done by computers and referred to as artificial intelligence.

Pattern recognition is more subtle than direct knowledge, such as touching a hot stove and realizing not to do that again, or knowing that 1 + 1 always equals 2. With pattern recognition, we retrieve *similar* situations and neurologically *estimate* the answer based on how this situation compares to prior experiences.

As you develop your mentor scorecard, identify the types of problems you expect to face, and then set your scorecard to search for people whose mental hard drive is filled with similar problems. For example, if you run a medium-sized construction business, the billionaire chairman of a media empire may have less in the way of pattern recognition than the vice president who operates a division of a trucking business.

Six Steps to Access Mentors

Six steps, if taken prior to talking to an advisor, will heighten the value of the interaction and help build the relationship. First, recognize that most people will give you a nearly unlimited quantity of 10-minute calls but have very little availability for an entire breakfast. The wiser strategy is to take advantage of shorter, high-impact interactions versus very few longer exchanges.

Second, prepare a set of notes before your discussion. They will help you organize your thoughts, which will shorten the time required to explain your question and maximize the time you have to listen and learn. John Elway was a classmate of mine and later played in five Super Bowls. He's also been an active entrepreneur and went on to build a successful auto franchise that was sold for $82 million. I love his statement: "I can't learn if I'm talking. The only way I can get better is to hear other people's opinions and find out why."[3]

Third, begin the conversation in the same way you would begin a well-run meeting: by articulating the problem you're trying to solve or the opportunity you're trying to capture. Do so explicitly, for example, "Katie, I want your advice on whether to . . ." Many times, I've listened intently to background information from someone calling for advice, only to realize that while I listened I was thinking about a different problem. By being explicit, your mentors will focus on the key issue, they'll limit their clarifying questions to what's relevant to your problem or opportunity, and their advice will specifically address what matters most to you.

Fourth, using your prepared notes offer only essential background information. While the situation may be new to you, your advisors will need less supplementary data than you think because of their pattern recognition, and they can always ask for additional information if necessary. I've been on many calls with people who spend nearly all the time providing background information, leaving only minutes at the end for me to offer my observations.

Fifth, offer your thoughts on what you believe you should do. Don't sell them on your recommendation—be clear that you want only to provide a starting point. You are not looking for reassurance. Make clear you have uncertainties, which is why you contacted them. But by pushing your own problem-solving skills, you will help frame the situation and over time this step will help improve your own pattern recognition.

Sixth, having taken the first five steps: shut up. Resist the urge to comment on everything they say, or offer time-consuming stories in response to their insights. This is the time to just concentrate and wrap your head around what they have to say.

Show Respect

An essential tool to creating the network that Kevin Taweel, Richard Branson, and Mary Barra described is expressing respect. You're asking for someone's time, which is the dearest asset they have. Instead of spending time with their family, their business, or their causes, they are giving their time to you. But mentorship is not a transactional relationship. You cannot repay them in the conventional sense. That's also not how they measure the relationship.

But you can show them respect by making careful use of their time. I recently received an email from a former student asking for my advice on designing a bonus plan. It included 31 bullet points supporting his recommendation. He had not taken the time to distill the issue to the essential data; he was leaving that to me.

A well-written email, organizing the critical background information, and Listening Like Joe are ways to signal that you appreciate their time. Instead of pressing "Send" immediately after you draft an email, tighten up the text to make sure your points are clearly expressed and efficiently presented. Avoid sending attachments that contain more information than they need. When you get together, have notes with you, to show that their time was worth an investment by you in preparation.

Finally, let them know how things turned out. They will be curious about the outcome. They understand you needed to process their advice side-by-side with your own judgment and that you may have taken a different path. But they are nonetheless interested in what happened.

A Final Thought . . .

The most important mentor in my life, Irv Grousbeck, frequently paraphrases the biblical passage: "We drink from wells we did not dig; we are warmed by fires we did not kindle." Seek out those people who understand that to the extent we've all enjoyed successes, they come with the help of others. You'll be fortunate to find those who mentor and offer advice as a recognition that they got to their place with the help of others.

The reference to the book of Deuteronomy can also be a beacon to illuminate your own path as your career progresses. While accumulating your own set of experiences, don't forget to recognize the new generation of leaders that, to use the phrase from coach Woody Hayes, you can help by "paying it forward."

Finding and Using Mentors

1. Identify people who can bring to your decision-making:
   a. *Objectivity* as faithfulness to the facts and self-awareness.
   b. *Pattern recognition* based on experiences similar to the problems and opportunities you are likely to face.

2. Access mentors purposefully:
   a. Take advantage of shorter, high-impact interactions.
   b. Prepare a set of notes before your discussion.
   c. Begin the conversation by articulating the problem you are trying to solve or opportunity you want to take advantage of.
   d. Offer only essential background information.
   e. Offer your ideas on what you believe you should do.
   f. Shut up. Maximize the time they have to provide feedback.

3. Say thank you by using your advisor's time efficiently and letting them know what happened.

4. When the time comes, pay it forward.

15 Executive Coaching

It is not what the coach knows; it is what his players have learned.

—Anonymous

My first direct experience with executive coaching was when the CEO of Sanku, Felix Brooks-church, asked whether the board would be agreeable to him hiring a coach. Since Felix had reported to me for half a dozen years before his promotion to CEO of the nonprofit I'd cofounded with Stephanie Cornell, I initially wondered why he wanted to hire an executive coach when he had me to ask for advice.

I posed the question to Eddie Poplawski, a former CEO and now a successful executive coach. Eddie explained to me why a coach is different from a mentor. A mentor is someone who can offer guidance from their own life experiences to help others address similar challenges. A mentor is often a role model, possessing characteristics that the mentee admires and hopes to emulate, who can help them find the answer to a question. A coach's job, on the other hand, is not to solve problems, but to build capability. A coach helps you figure out who you want to be, where you want to go, and how you would like to get there. "Coaches don't drive the car," as Eddie explained. "They sit beside you in the front seat as you choose the roads you want to travel."

What Is a Coach?

In her 1885 novel, *Mrs. Dymond,* Anne Isabella Thackeray Richie popularized the phrase: *If you give a man a fish, you feed him for a day. Teach him to fish, and you feed him for a lifetime.* Coaches teach you to fish. Their mission is to help you build leadership skills, not create a dependency. A coach participates in your development by creating frameworks for solving business problems, not by handing you the answer.

A coach is also free of a personal stake in the outcome. In my relationship with Felix, I had my own baggage as he was following in my footsteps as the previous CEO. Felix needed to take the organization on a path that would at times diverge from what I thought best. He needed my advice, but he also needed a resource with whom he could talk freely about any aspect of the business or his situation—including his relationship with me. Eddie summed it up in this way, "Where else in your life do you have a skilled, supportive, and unbiased resource in your corner who has no stake in your outcomes, and whose only desire is to support you in your quest to be the best version of yourself?"

A coach creates a safe space in which you can wander and wonder as you explore new opportunities, expand your possibilities, and examine how you feel about your personal and professional circumstances. Still, don't expect a coach to serve as your personal advocate. Their job is to support you as you build the subskills and wisdom that will help you maximize your performance as a manager. Sometimes that means telling you what you don't want to hear. For the very reason that they have only your interests in mind, they are not your buddy or your promoter.

Finding the Right Coach

One study found that two-thirds of all failed coaching relationships were due to a mismatch between the coach and the client—not the coaching process itself.[1] To find the right coach, begin by creating a list of potential coaches. Search engines will lead you to a large list of candidates, but the preferred method is to tap into your network by asking other managers, as well as lawyers, accountants, and active investors, for their recommendations.

Next, check the coach's formal training. Coaching is a skill, not an accumulation of life experiences. The International Coaching Federation (ICF) and the World Association of Business Coaches provide credentialling for coaches, programs, certifications, and accreditation. Major universities such as Georgetown University School of Continuing Studies now offer an executive certificate in leadership coaching.

Next, meet with two or three coaches before deciding, to get a sense of the range of options, styles, and experiences available to you. Someone who has worked mostly with CEOs may be less equipped to guide a division leader of a large corporation. The same reasoning suggests that a coach with a great deal of experience with entrepreneurs may be better suited for someone in the start-up phase of a company. Similarly, if your organization includes multiple family members, you may want to match yourself with someone who has experience in family-owned and operated organizations.

In these conversations, you'll want to ask them how often they would expect to meet with you and for how long, how they handle emergency sessions, and whether they are available for unexpected situations. Ask to what extent they are open to remote sessions.

Just as the best athletic coaches are often not the best players, so too with executive coaches. Coaching is about managing a *process*. Bill Campbell, the subject of the book *Trillion Dollar Coach*,[2] never thought of himself as better at management than his long-time client Eric Schmidt, former CEO of Google, or any of the other Silicon Valley rock stars he coached. Instead, he created a process in which they could become the best versions of themselves.

Which is also why your coach doesn't need to be an expert in your industry. They are not business consultants with subject matter expertise. While consulting projects may involve leadership training, a coaching relationship is designed to focus on the skills and capabilities of you as an individual.

Chemistry matters, but not in the sense of kinship. You are not hiring a friend, but you need to feel comfortable talking with them about your personal life, health issues, and other pressures. This is not to say your coach is a doctor or psychotherapist. Nonetheless, the best coaches need to understand your particular context, and you must be able to share that context with them in order to receive their best work. Personal issues inevitably have a presence in your work life.

According to work at Stanford and the University of California, 72% of entrepreneurs struggle with mental health concerns, such as depression or bipolar disorder, and many struggle with outside dependencies.[3] If you don't feel you can disclose issues in your marriage or use of alcohol, for example, then keep looking. If you have a less conventional arrangement with your family or partner, or if you have a unique relationship with someone at work, if you come from a background that is underrepresented within your company or industry, consider discussing this with potential coaches and getting a sense of any prior experiences with these areas and how they have approached them in the past.

Because of these dynamics, confidentiality is a critical component to the experience, but not in the same sense as with a doctor or clergy. Confidentiality means that you have control over the information. While about 60% of CEOs choose to keep the coaching relationship completely private,[4] nearly a third use *controlled confidentiality*, which means their coach may share curated information with your constituents as you authorize, in order to maximize your growth and development.

The Coaching Process

The legendary business thinker Peter Drucker, who is often credited with being the first "executive coach," said, "My greatest strength as a [coach] is to be ignorant and ask a few questions." A coach generally uses questions more than statements to guide you. As Eddie told me, their purpose is to be with you as you grapple with the problems yourself, asking probing and thoughtful questions that help you build your capacity and *pattern recognition*. Which is why you should beware of anyone who seems to use a formulaic approach or a process that is universally applied to all clients. Your coach should understand where you want to go in your particular journey, and then what skills or behaviors you need to get to the place you chose.

In a typical coaching relationship, you'll meet twice a month for one to one-and-a-half hours, whether in person or remotely. You share responsibility for the agenda, so it's important to go in with a sense of the goals, issues, challenges, and aspirations that you hope to achieve. Some executives put off getting a coach because of the time it takes to prepare for these sessions. But a good coach will also help you become a fanatical custodian of time, helping you make your weeks more productive and your calendar less chaotic, more than offsetting the time you spend together.

As part of the process, you may have your coach spend time with your staff, supervisor, board of directors, or other constituents. This was the case when Felix began his coaching relationship. When Felix's coach called me, she asked my opinions about Felix's opportunities, his blind spots, as well as his superpowers. But she used my opinions only as data to combine with observations she made from others she spoke with. She also politely dug into what biases I brought to the relationship, for example probing to get a sense of how I dealt with Felix making decisions that contrasted with my tenure running Sanku.

Some coaches will, if you request, hold you accountable for progress on projects or initiatives that you're working on. That accountability might be an incentive to meet your deadlines, but ultimately the best coaches will help you build your own capacity for accountability, identifying the roadblocks you face in meeting deadlines, and helping you devise solutions so that you don't need a third party going forward to help you hit your targets.

Some larger companies offer internal coaching for their employees. Internal coaches have the advantage of knowing how things are done in their organization, but the big shortcoming of this approach is that it violates two tenets of coaching: *controlled confidentiality* and working with someone with no agenda beyond your success. No matter how carefully internal coaches follow the rules for confidentiality, they are still an employee of the organization you work for. A better alternative is for companies to offer and subsidize independent coaching as an employee benefit.

Expect to pay a fee that can range from a few hundred dollars per session to multiples of that. Nonetheless the return on investment (ROI) can be enormous. In one study, a quarter of companies believed the return on their coaching was up to 49 times the cost of the fees, and a separate study showed an average ROI for coaching that was seven times the initial investment.[5]

A good coach is an investment, not an expense. Before taking a cheaper option, evaluate the price difference against the benefit of making a series of improved leadership decisions over time.

Group or Peer Coaching

Group or peer coaching is an alternative to a conventional coaching relationship. Two of the best-known organizations that help business leaders grow through group or peer coaching are the Young Presidents Organization (YPO) and Vistage. YPO sets a minimum size for the organization and requires members to be under the age of 45 when they join. Vistage also has membership requirements, although not as restrictive. The coaching formats for both organizations are similar. In a confidential setting, and using a structured format, members present issues or opportunities to groups of approximately 12. To facilitate the process, the organizations generally avoid having two competitors in the same small group, and they discourage group members from being in business arrangements together.

For most of my professional life I was a member of YPO, and I found the experience valuable. What the YPO approach offers that you can't get with a single coach is the richness of multiple points of view. Yet I found two shortcomings with peer coaching. The first is that the group members, while well-intended, are not trained in coaching. This often means that they give feedback that sounds more like advice than coaching, and are less focused on building capability and more on solving the presented problem. Also, because there is a social component to YPO and Vistage, members have a stake in the relationship and care about your impression of them. For this reason, group members may be less open about their own vulnerabilities despite the confidential nature of the forum.

Secondly, the format limits you to a small number of presentations. If a 12-person group meets 10 times a year and has the capacity to work on three issues per meeting, that suggests a capacity to tackle only about three of your presentations per year. While any well-functioning group will accommodate emergencies, most of your needs won't get anywhere near the time you'd receive with a coaching relationship that meets twice a month and focuses exclusively on your situation.

A Final Thought . . .

The days when people viewed coaching as a way to save a flailing executive are over. Former Google CEO Eric Schmidt said that the best advice he ever received was to "have a coach." Think of a coach the way a star athlete does—as an essential component to reaching your full potential.

Felix was wise enough to recognize that he needed someone who was *not* the organization's founder, and would work with him intensively and aggressively to expand his capabilities. After he hired a coach, I saw him make the transition from my employee to an independent leader. He became comfortable asking for advice, but then making his own decision based on my judgment as well as the other inputs he received.

It also improved our relationship professionally and personally. I sensed that his coach guided him on identifying ways that I could be useful, which Felix modeled in our interactions, making me a better chairman. Interestingly, we spend more time working together on issues now, not less. The coach was not a replacement or substitute for me, but instead an essential addition to the Sanku team.

Executive Coaching

1. A coach's job is not to solve problems, but to build capability. Their mission is to help you build leadership skills, not create a dependency.

2. Choosing a coach:
   a. Create a list of potential coaches using online searches and tapping into your network for recommendations.
   b. Weigh heavily whether the candidate has had formal training.
   c. Meet with three coaches to get a sense of the range of options, styles, and experiences.
   d. They don't need to be an expert in your industry.

3. Find someone with whom you feel comfortable talking about your personal life, health issues, and other pressures.

4. Use controlled confidentiality. At your discretion, your coach may share information with your constituents to maximize your growth and development.

5. Beware of anyone who uses a formulaic approach or a process that is universally applied to all clients.

6. Group or peer coaching provides the richness of multiple points of view, but peers are not trained in coaching and often try to solve problems instead of building capacity. As well, the format limits you to a small number of presentations.

Ten Questions to Ask a Prospective Coach

1. How many clients do you currently have, and what is your total capacity?

2. How many years have you coached, and why did you decide to make this your vocation?

3. What percentage of your clients have similar-sized organizations to mine, are in a similar age and stage of leadership to mine or as me, and what percentage of those clients work with organizations with similar structure to mine (for example: nonprofit, investor-owned, or family-operated)?

4. How are you compensated?

5. Are the sessions in person or remote? How often do you like to meet and how long is a typical session?

6. How do you structure the sessions, and how is the subject matter determined?

7. I have struggled with [alcohol, bipolar, marriage, etc.]. What is your experience with these issues?

8. Tell me about any formal training you have had and what you learned from that training.

9. What do you think makes for the best coach/client relationships?

10. Describe for me a recent situation where the coaching relationship failed and what you and the client learned from that failure.

16 A Board of Advisors

She generally gave herself very good advice (though she very seldom followed it).

—Lewis Carroll, *Alice in Wonderland*

Laura Franklin leads a company that operates clinics for children on the autism spectrum. I've been on her board since she began, and in one particular meeting I expressed my view about how to expand to new markets. Laura jotted down a note, and then proceeded to the next agenda item as if I had the final say. But before she could do so, another board member jumped in with an alternative view. Then, as a group, we considered the two approaches, eventually settling on a third alternative. We never would have come up with that ultimate idea had it not been for the *ideation* and *creativity* that only exists inside a group dynamic.

One-on-one conversations with mentors and advisors cannot replace the ideation and creativity that takes place when you convene advisors and set them loose on your problem or opportunity. Group versus individual advice accomplishes different objectives, and one is not a substitute for the other.

Some managers see the board as only a necessary evil, one that encroaches upon their autonomy and decision-making power, perhaps even an existential threat to their job. Fixated by horror stories that are passed along among entrepreneurs, they prefer to "maintain control" for as long as possible—but at too high of a price.

The solution is not to avoid a board, or advisory group, but instead to correctly organize and manage it. Your relationship with your board members doesn't have to be antagonistic or create uncomfortable power dynamics. If you select the right people and run the meetings as a problem-solving forum, you'll unleash a powerful force in ideation and creativity that will accelerate your success and enhance, not diminish, your authority.

If you're running a nonprofit, a community program, or a unit within a larger organization, you might not have the option to put together a formal board of directors, but you can still create an equivalently effective and invaluable panel of advisors. For this chapter, though, I'll refer to this broader definition simply as a "board."

Selecting Board Members

At Stanford, we studied an early entrepreneur who considered offering a board seat to an investor who helped him secure bank financing. When the entrepreneur told his father about the potential board member, the father said, "You don't need someone who can help you get a bank loan. You need someone who can show you how to run a company." In his own way, the father was pointing out that his son was using the wrong scorecard.

Just like in hiring, identifying great board members begins by developing a scorecard that is limited to around five key criteria and developed using the same subskills already applied in hiring and in identifying advisors.

Next, create a list of potential board members from your network that may fit the scorecard you created. Be generous with who you add, as you can always take people off the list later, but initially it's better to brainstorm broadly. As you do so, it's best to exclude suppliers and employees as you'll need the flexibility to discuss and make decisions that may at times run contrary to their personal interests. Then, compare that list against your scorecard (Figure 16.1):

Criteria	Standard	How Will I Know?
Relevant board experience	Three or more prior boards with private companies	LinkedIn Asking candidate
Evidence of adding value on boards	80% of chief executive officers positively refer them as a board member	References: *Would you have them again? *Can you give me an example of . . . ?
Relevant operating experience	Five or more years as a senior manager of an operating company	LinkedIn Asking candidate
Willingness to travel	Able to make 80% of board meetings in-person	References from prior boards
Able to offer unique opinions but work as a team	Does not automatically agree with others, provides unique insights, but able to move forward as a team	References: *Can you give me an example of . . . ? *Were there times when . . . ?

Figure 16.1 Board Scorecard

In most situations, a formal interviewing process is awkward. It might also damage your relationship with anyone you don't eventually invite to your board. Where it becomes necessary to get data directly from potential board members, spend time with them informally by asking them for advice. If you already have a board, invite them to a meeting as an expert guest, and observe how they interact. Finally, take advantage of informal reference checks, using the skills from Chapter 1 to diplomatically compare the person against your scorecard.

One-Quarter Rule

In my early days as an entrepreneur, I structured my board meeting agendas around updates of each functional area. I awarded nearly equal time to each department, regardless of the priorities of the organization. Next, I added a discussion of any current dumpster fires, most of which had little consequence to building long-term value. Lastly, for "show and tell," I often described initiatives or company accomplishments of which I was proud. Instead, I should have used that time to tap into their wisdom and address the toughest problems, or the greatest opportunities, I was facing.

Over time, I came to organize my agenda using the *one-quarter rule*. Allocate the first quarter of your agenda to updating the board on what has happened, as base-knowledge for later problem solving. Using techniques from Chapter 11 (Seven Steps to Running a Great Meeting), much of this can be done by providing written information in advance.

The next quarter of the meeting should be devoted to problems you are working on, or opportunities that you want to take advantage of, that reside in the upper row of the Eisenhower matrix (Figure 16.2), careful not to focus too much time on the "urgent" quadrant. The "important" and "not urgent" quadrant is almost always where your board can help create the most value for your organization.

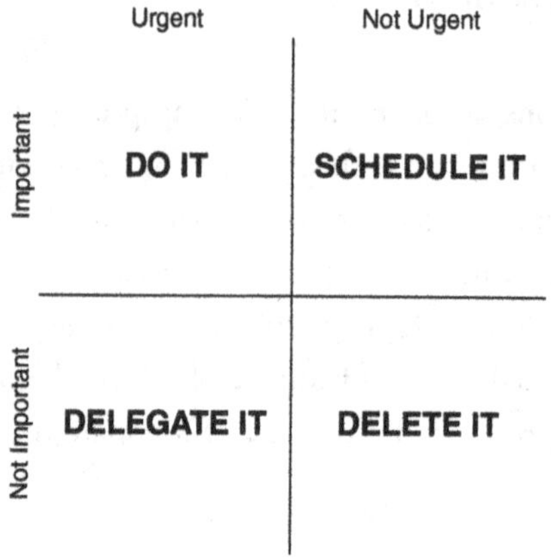

Figure 16.2 The Eisenhower Matrix

For the next quarter of the agenda, create a list of standing topics that are key drivers to long-term value, which you will cycle through every two years. The list will vary depending on your industry and situation, but they share characteristics with areas of your organization that may not face a particular problem or opportunity, but benefit from foundational discussion.

For example, a software company might choose to periodically discuss its product roadmap, while a nonprofit might want to annually review its fundraising strategy. As a starting point, consider these five areas of focus for your standing topics:

- Team and Leadership
- Product Quality
- Competitive Analysis
- Supplier Analysis
- Pricing and Switching Costs

For instance, as it pertains to Team and Leadership, this is the opportunity to move beyond the shiny objects such as someone quitting or an urgent compensation matter, to an in-depth discussion of your team. Here you'll address long-term matters such as training, new ways to organize the company, strategic compensation, competitive recruitment, and what you need to do to keep your winners.

No matter how hard we try, the urgent has a nagging tendency to preempt the important. Avoid the tyranny of the urgent by using guardrails to create a standing schedule that addresses one or two of the standing topics. For example (Figure 16.3):

	Q1	Q2	Q3	Q4
Even Year	Product Quality	Competitive Analysis	Pricing and Switching Costs	Team and Leadership
Odd Year	Product Quality	Competitive Analysis	Supplier Analysis	Team and Leadership
Even Year	Product Quality	Competitive Analysis	Pricing and Switching Costs	Team and Leadership
Odd Year	Product Quality	Competitive Analysis	Supplier Analysis	Team and Leadership

Figure 16.3 Strategic Board Schedule

This was driven home for me when I led a regional chain of auto parts stores. I had played down the threats from my competitors as they surrounded me. My head deep in the sand, I never used my board as a forum to objectively test and challenge my assumptions. Had I used them proactively, I would have seen the threat for what it was and charted a path into markets where we could have succeeded, instead of eventually having to sell my company to one of those very competitors.

For the final quarter of the agenda, schedule nothing. A common mistake is to pack the meeting with as much content as possible in a mistaken effort to maximize the value of the meeting. But doing so invariably leaves no "white space" for board members to raise issues you might not have planned to discuss (like the discussion we had with Laura over how to expand her chain of clinics). Ideation and creativity cannot happen when the clock is ticking loudly, everyone feels rushed, and there is no time to take the discussion on unexpected detours.

Running the Meeting

Your job is to facilitate ideation and creation, not present material and respond to questions. Put another way, you are the conductor of the orchestra while the board members play the music. And much like the six-part framework for managing a conversation with an advisor, there is a set of four steps to follow that will guarantee the best result in a board meeting.

1: State Your Objective

Begin by articulating the objective: what winning looks like. This begins by using the same skills of running a good management meeting by stating as clearly and simply as possible the problem you are trying to solve or the opportunity you want to take advantage of.

Next, you'll need to clarify what you want from them, and that falls into four categories: *advice*, *decision*, *approval*, or *background*. Be clear which of these you are asking of them. For example, if you are looking for *advice*, this signals to your board that they should focus on testing your thinking, offering frameworks, challenging your assumptions, bringing their experience and pattern recognition to the matter, while refraining from offering comments that may be construed as instructions.

As you articulate the objective and the board's role, use unambiguous language. For instance, here is the same objective stated under each of the four categories:

Advice: _"Before I make my decision, I'd like advice on how to think about whether to raise prices on our smaller customers."_

Decision: _"We need to decide as a board whether to raise prices on our smaller customers."_

Approval: _"I want your approval to move forward on raising prices for our smaller customers."_

Background: _"I raised the prices on our smaller customers. I wanted you to understand why I did so."_

2: Ask for Clarifying Questions

Because _everyone is entitled to their own opinion, but not their own facts,_ before the discussion ask for clarifying questions from each board member. Examples of clarifying questions are: "How are you defining a 'smaller' customer?" "What do our competitors charge for the same service?" or "When was the last time we raised prices?"

Managing this step in a board meeting is not the same as for one of your management meetings. Let's face it, board members are less easy to train than your staff. To prevent the board's conversation from shifting to a discussion, begin by being specific and avoid any subtlety. For example: "Before we get into the meat of the discussion, I want to make sure everyone understands the material. In service to that, I want to first ask for clarifying questions, and then we will get into the discussion. Charlie, let's begin with you. What clarifying questions do you have?"

Make it clear that you'll be coming around to everyone so that each person can listen, knowing they don't have to hunt for the moment to jump in with their own clarifying questions. If someone strays into a discussion, which will happen, you might say, "Melinda, that's worth some further discussion. If we can hold for a second, as soon as we complete our clarifying questions, I'll shift to the observation you just shared." Then write it down. The mere fact that you are making a written note will reassure Melinda that you plan to return to her observation.

3: Facilitate a Discussion

It's your job to manage a discussion that brings out the best ideation and creativity from the board. A major challenge, though, is that you have a finite amount of time to do so. Which is why you should not eat up any minutes restating anything that was already provided in the advance reading material. If you need to supplement any of the information, speak from a set of prepared notes. Organizing your thoughts in advance will drastically shorten the amount of time you need to communicate the material.

Next, as the discussion unfolds, avoid the temptation to respond to every comment. You don't need to opine to each thing that is said. Doing so draws away the energy as you force each member to listen to you comment on everything said, turning the meeting into an interview of you, not a forum for ideation and creativity. You'll also be a better listener if you don't feel the need to formulate a response to whatever is being said. As Steven R. Covey warned, "Most people do not listen with the intent to understand; they listen with the intent to reply." Most critically, it cuts off any back-and-forth among your board. You know you're succeeding when your board members are talking among themselves and you're absorbing and learning, not responding.

As you conduct your orchestra, make sure you hear all the instruments. If one board member is less vocal, draw that person into the conversation with something such as, "Sharon, I imagine you saw similar situations at Wellington. How do you come down on this?"

Finally, it is important that you keep the conversation on track. Your board will appreciate the occasional re-direction back to the problem you are trying to solve or the opportunity you want to seize. If a promising but unrelated topic is raised, you can move it to the "parking lot" for further discussion by saying, "I want to make sure we first get resolution on the price increase, so let me jot that down, and we'll circle back to that at the end of the meeting if time permits."

4: Close the Loop

Before moving on to the next agenda topic, make clear what you believe was decided or agreed to—especially if the conversation involved lively and active back-and-forth among the board members where people's points of view might have changed or been modified. For example:

Advice: "I received the guidance I need to make my decision on whether to raise prices. What I heard from the board is that . . ."

Decision: "I understand we agreed to raise prices on our smaller customers by 7.4%."

Approval: "I understand I have your approval to raise prices on the smaller customers by 7.4%."

Background: "My goal was to give you clarity and background on the implications and reasons why I raised prices by 7.4%. Are there any further questions?"

Despite how clear you may have been during the meeting, misunderstandings are inevitable. After the meeting send a short email listing what was agreed to, which will essentially be a restatement of your verbal summary. In doing so, prioritize speed over form. Memories fade quickly, and it is better to have a rough email sent within an hour of the meeting than a polished summary that goes out days later. If there are to-do items, future deliverables, or assignments to any board members, here is the place to document those.

A Final Thought . . .

When I was a chief executive officer, as I gained experience I learned to ask myself a simple question after each meeting: "Will I do anything differently because of the meeting?" The purpose of my meetings was not to convince the board that I was on the right track but to seek and take advice in a setting that facilitated ideation and creativity. Over time I learned to bring them hard problems to solve and big opportunities to examine, rather than show off my performance or bore them with unactionable background information. This one simple question, whether I will do anything differently as a result of the time together, averted the temptation to make those meetings victory laps or history lessons. It forced me to conduct the meeting in a way that facilitated ideation and creativity, which then led to building value.

A Board of Advisors

1. Convene multiple advisors together and set them loose on your problem or opportunity to generate *ideation* and *creativity*.

2. Steps to identifying board members:
   a. Limit your scorecard to about five key criteria.
   b. Create a list of potential board members from your network.
   c. Spend time with them informally, asking them for advice.
   d. If you have a board, invite them to a meeting as an expert guest and observe how they interact.
   e. Take advantage of informal reference checks.

3. Set your agenda using the *one-quarter rule*:
   a. Updates required to understand the organization's status.
   b. Important problems selected from the top row of the Eisenhower matrix.
   c. Standing topics (e.g., Team and Leadership, Product Quality).
   d. White space for impromptu topics or expanded discussion.

4. Running the meeting:
   a. State your objective and their role: seeking advice, making a decision, receiving permission, or providing background.
   b. Ask for *clarifying questions*.
   c. Facilitate a discussion as an orchestra conductor, making sure all the instruments have a chance to be heard.

5. Avoid the temptation to respond to every comment. Your job is to facilitate ideation and creativity among the members.

6. Close the loop at the end of each topic to make sure you have alignment.

PART IV
Setting and Adhering to Priorities

17 Key Performance Indicators

Knowledge is knowing a tomato is a fruit. Wisdom is not putting it in a fruit salad.

—Miles Kington

Chandos Mahon operates one of the largest rubber recycling companies in the country. Each year, his company processes more than two hundred million pounds of rubber, which they recycle into by-products such as playground material and fuel to make electricity. They operate an international shipping port, multiple processing plants, and a large truck fleet.

For years, Chandos' business grew, but his profits remained flat. It seemed the added revenue was always offset by an increasingly complex company to manage. Chandos asked me if I'd help with this problem, and so I had him send me the data he uses to manage his business. He emailed me three spreadsheets that included columns and rows of dense historical data describing events from the past. But there were no key performance indicators (KPIs) to help him make forward-facing decisions. From what I saw, I wasn't surprised that the company was having trouble making money.

I see this a lot with early leaders, and it's because many of us begin our professional lives measured mostly by how well we collect and present historical data. These ingrained habits are hard to change. As a former student told me:

> In my prior jobs, I was creating big reports, crunching data, and doing "research." That was how I was valued. But I discovered that it had little to do with running things. I needed to focus myself and the company on where we were going, not explaining where we had been. I needed to understand the difference between historical data and actionable information.

For three months, a Harvard Business School team tracked, in 15-minute increments, how 27 top performing CEOs spent their time, accumulating more than 60,000 hours of data.[1] A key observation was that they all had simple KPI "dashboards." They wanted the straightforward facts, simplified, and in a version that they could share with their team to make decisions that would impact future results. But it is easy to confuse KPIs with historical data, and understanding the distinction begins with finding the right altitude.

Finding the Right Altitude

I challenged Chandos to answer a simple question: "If you were to succeed at only one thing, and ignore everything else, what would it be?" My question ran counter to his habits of perfectionism. He didn't understand why I insisted on only one thing, but he played along. A few weeks later he told me that the most important thing was sales. But he was flying at too high an altitude.[2]

Which is why I then asked Chandos about the best way to make sales go up. He said that the easiest way was to have customers love his service. His thesis was this simple: if his customers were happy, they would buy more of what he had to sell and be less likely to switch to a competitor. Happy customers meant more sales. Now we were getting somewhere. Given this information, I suggested he talk to his customers using the five questions from Chapter 13 (Five Questions).

Through those questions he discovered one thing that really made his customers happy. With this understanding we designed a KPI that focused his operations around that one thing. He later added a second and third KPI to his operation, and now runs his day-to-day business off only three numbers. He later told me:

> *My instinct was to collect everything. In retrospect that was easier than figuring out a few impactful things to track. But after we figured it out, the path forward became straightforward. Today every team member knows our three KPIs. We live to hit those numbers and have set profit records ever since.*

Material. Actionable. Measurable.

In a conversation at a bar in Palo Alto, Herb Kelleher, the founder and former CEO of Southwest Airlines, described to me how just one KPI saved his company. He told me the story of the spring of 1972, when his company was down to $143 in its checking account and to survive, it had to sell one of only four planes it owned. Charging customers less money than American Airlines in his core Texas market, it seemed, was not a formula for sustainability if the airline didn't have a cost structure that made money at those prices.

To be viable, Southwest Airlines had to get its passengers and bags off a landed plane, restock the refreshments, board the plane for the next flight, and pull away from the gate all in 10 minutes. "Airplanes only make money in the air," Kelleher explained. The entire company came to live for one KPI, which they called the 10-Minute Turn, and it saved his airline because the KPI was *material, actionable,* and *measurable*.

The 10-Minute Turn was *material* because it allowed his planes to be in the air more. That meant they made a lot more money. It was *actionable* because it led to real-time operational decisions. For example, instead of waiting until the plane was empty and then bringing in a cleaning crew, flight attendants began cleaning up as the last departing passengers moved toward the front of the plane. By the time the pilot said goodbye to the last passenger, the plane was almost entirely cleaned. The 10-Minute Turn was *measurable* because anyone with a wristwatch could calculate the amount of time the plane had been parked at the gate.

Historical financial statements seldom drive operational decisions. Yet Harvard professors Christopher Ittner and David Larcker observed that only 23% of companies identified opportunities to succeed through nonfinancial performance in the way Kelleher had.[3] While Southwest's competitors were mired in reviewing quarterly earnings, Kelleher's company managed according to a single KPI that was material, actionable, and measurable. In so doing, he clobbered American Airlines.

Duplication. Simplicity. Frequency. Format.

To unleash the power of a KPI, they need to be understood and used by your frontline workers. Too often KPIs are saved for the boardroom and senior leadership team. But those are not the people making daily decisions that impact how fast your plane leaves the gate. Your frontline team is your primary audience of a KPI. To take advantage of this, you need to apply a fidelity to *duplication, simplicity, frequency,* and *format.*

Duplication

When it comes to communicating KPIs to your team, less is more. Begin by eliminating overlapping KPIs. To illustrate the point, imagine you run a call center. If you know that 80% of dropped calls are the result of on-hold times, you don't need metrics for both on-hold time and dropped calls. If you reduce the on-hold time, the dropped calls will also come down. As well, the solution to dropped calls is likely the same operational solution to address long on-hold times. By choosing one or the other, you accomplish almost the same while creating clarity around a single KPI. Understand that KPIs are not about precisely measuring all aspects of your operation, but tools to guide forward-facing management decisions.

Simplicity

Today, our ability to collect and process data is so potent that we can create complex KPIs that your frontline organization could never understand.

Returning to the prior example, we might use a mathematical average of the on-hold time, with a target of 45 seconds. That's simple. The problem is we'd get the same result from both of these five sets of calls:

48, 51, 26, 76, 46 = average of 49 seconds

32, 17, 41, 24, 132 = average of 49 seconds

In the first instance, only one call was within the target of 45 seconds, indicating a systemic issue. In the second case, a single call threw off the entire average. Solving for a systemic issue versus an exception would call for different approaches.

One solution might be to calculate the standard deviation, which shows the spread between the lowest and the highest number.[4] Standard deviation is calculated using the following formula:

$$f(x) = \frac{1}{\sigma\sqrt{2\pi}} e^{-\frac{1}{2}\left(\frac{x-\mu}{\sigma}\right)^2}$$

But this is a call for simplicity, not PhD mathematics. Returning to the example of Southwest Airlines, Kelleher could have had his KPI as the breakdown of the percentage of time the plane was in the air, at the terminal, and idle, as compared to a standard that varied based on time of day and congestion at the airport. That would have been a more accurate calculation of asset utilization. It also would not have saved his airline as it would have left every baggage handler and gate agent scratching their heads.

Returning to our call center, a better solution is to sacrifice some precision and use a KPI that everyone can understand. For instance, how many calls fall within an acceptable standard. That would be easily understood, it solves for the systemic versus exceptional issue, and every member of the call center staff now only needs to understand one simple KPI: what percentage of the calls came in under 45 seconds.

*48, 51, **26**, 76, **46** = 20% of calls within standard*

***32, 17, 41, 24,** 132 = 80% of calls within standard*

Frequency

The frequency with which you communicate a KPI should be based on the speed at which your organization can act on the information, not how often you can collect the data. If on-hold issues are principally addressed with staffing, and that is managed in the bi-monthly plan, then issue a twice monthly KPI report before each staffing plan is created. If, on the other hand, team members react throughout the day by shifting from nonurgent work to answering inbound calls, then the data might be best viewed on a minute-by-minute basis.

Because collecting data comes at a cost, start conservatively, collecting the data on a less-frequent cadence than you might think. As you do so, note whether the operational changes you make would have improved if the information had arrived more frequently. Increase or decrease the frequency until the communication of your KPIs lines up with your ability to act on that data.

Format

Elaborate formatting comes at a cost. While your call center managers are generating impressive charts and preparing elaborate PowerPoint presentations, they could be coaching employees, sourcing new hires, or patiently talking to upset customers. Top performing leaders have no patience for office theater that produces visually attractive graphics and colorful presentations, but adds nothing to the underlying content. They also understand that it's not enough for them to be a fanatical custodian of their time; so too does their entire team. In Southwest Airline's example, the format was . . . a single number.

A Final Thought . . .

It was an achievement when Herb Kelleher identified the connection between turnaround time and profitability. But that alone would have had no impact on Southwest Airlines. The genius of Kelleher's leadership was his ability to get the entire organization to rally around a single KPI. He supplemented his KPI with recognition, excitement, and reward. It allowed the team to make operational choices that got their airplanes in the air and take pride in doing so.

In celebrating their 50th anniversary, Southwest Airlines wrote how the 10-Minute Turn saved them from bankruptcy and then transformed their company into the most consistently profitable airline in history:[5]

What became known as the 10-Minute Turn was an all-hands-on-deck operation. In the breakroom, it often looked like a fire drill when word came in that an aircraft was arriving. Lunch pails slammed shut, conversations halted mid-sentence, and everyone raced to their posts. More than 100 tasks had to be completed before the plane could depart, and a delay in even one could derail the entire operation. This meant that nobody—not the pilots, not the provisioning agents, not even Herb Kelleher himself—was above taking out the trash or restocking peanuts.

Key Performance Indicators

1. The best leaders want straightforward facts in a version they can share with their team to make decisions that impact future results.

2. Begin by asking yourself: "If we could succeed at only one thing, and ignore everything else, what would it be?"

3. Measure each potential KPI against three tests:

   - Material

   - Actionable

   - Measurable

4. Format the KPI to the audience and the frontline team that needs to make operating decisions. Keep in mind the following concepts:

   - Duplication

   - Simplicity

   - Frequency

   - Format

5. The genius of a KPI is the ability to get the entire organization to rally around a single goal.

18 The Operating Plan

Give me six hours to chop down a tree and I will spend the first four sharpening the axe.

—Abraham Lincoln

Mike Flint had been Warren Buffett's pilot for over a decade and was thinking about the next chapter in his career. When he asked his boss for some advice, Buffet told him to write down his top 25 life goals. A few days later, Flint showed him the list. Buffett barely glanced at it. Instead, he told Flint to circle the top five. When Flint finished, Buffet told him, "Everything you didn't circle just became your *Avoid-At-All-Cost* list. These things get no attention from you until you've succeeded with your top five."

The lesson from Buffet is that prioritizing is not saying "no" to *unattractive* ideas. Prioritization is a willingness to also say "no" to the *attractive* ideas. But this is difficult for ambitious and creative managers because they make the mistake of thinking that their whole list could get completed if only their organization could keep up with all their ideation. The problem with this is that the pace at which you come up with good ideas will always outrun your organization's ability to implement them. It's not because your team is incapable of moving fast. It's that while ideation can happen on the drive home from work, implementation requires concrete acts like hiring people, buying equipment, identifying suppliers, and integrating these initiatives into your accounting systems—all while running the existing business.

Because of this tension between ambition and realism, prioritization requires a process—discarding so many great ideas seldom happens on its own, and a process of institutional prioritization begins with the annual *operating plan*.

An operating plan is not a budget. A budget is a prediction of future financial results and by itself has limited value. An operating plan is an articulation of the goals and priorities for the coming year, metrics to measure progress, and a roadmap on how to get from here to there. An operating plan focuses the organization on a set of priorities, shapes forward-facing decisions, and aligns the stakeholders and the management around a tactical plan.

Generating Opportunities

Begin by creating a *baseline budget*, which represents what the team believes will occur without implementing any new initiatives.[1] Put another way, it is how the company will perform if everyone just keeps doing what they're currently doing.

Suppose last year you opened two new locations, and those locations will add 15% to next year's revenue. The baseline budget includes this projected increase in revenue. The baseline budget separates what has already been put in place from what you may add as new initiatives. The baseline budget doesn't require a high degree of detail or precision and can include just your income statement and projected KPIs.

With the baseline budget in hand, the next step is for your leadership team to brainstorm ideas for the following year. Be sure to stretch the team's creative energy, broadening the process beyond the most outspoken, or senior, members by making sure to solicit everyone's views. An easy technique for this is described in Chapter 11 (Seven Steps to Running a Great Meeting) by having people speak in reverse order of seniority.

As part of the process, consider what you learned from the five questions you asked your employees, customers, suppliers, and competitors. And as you manage the group, use concepts introduced in Chapter 16 (A Board of Advisors) and Chapter 11 (Seven Steps to Running a Great Meeting) to maximize the pace of *ideation* and *creation*.

Once you develop a set of potential initiatives for the following year, eliminate those with limited promise and focus on developing what remains by fleshing out enough tactical detail to get a sense of the effort involved and the approximate cost. For example, let's assume one such idea was to create an inside sales effort. Quickly create a list of the major steps and associated cost and revenue. Your whiteboard might look like:

Inside sales effort:

> *Hire a sales manager to report to Lizzie*
>
> *Scott hires 2–3 inside reps to expand business with current customers*
>
> *This frees up existing reps to work on new business with Katie*
>
> *Cost = $75K (manager), $45k each rep*
>
> *Revenue = $200k revenue per rep, 45% gross margin*
>
> *6 months ramp up*

Once you're down to a few promising initiatives and have listed the major steps and financial implications, summarize the ideas in a grid (Figure 18.1).

Now, Cross Almost Everything Off the List

As part of Apple's annual planning process, Steve Jobs would take 100 of his top managers on an annual retreat to generate the following year's opportunities. Once the list was complete, Jobs would announce: "We can only do three."[2] Everything else on the board became Apple's version of an Avoid-At-All-Cost list. To reinforce this, throughout the year, Jobs would routinely ask members of his leadership team, "How many things have you said no to today?" Long-time design chief Jony Ive said of Apple's approach, "Focus means saying no to something that you [think]—with every bone in your body—is a phenomenal idea."[3]

The reassuring news is that it if you're wrong, while it's hard to subtract it's easy to add. A company that takes on too many initiatives and needs to subtract will almost always first push the organization too hard in an effort to succeed, wearing down the team, lowering morale, and diffusing focus before finally acknowledging defeat. In contrast if you find yourself ahead of schedule

	Initiative A	Initiative B	Initiative C	Initiative D	Initiative E	Initiative F	Initiative G	Initiative H
Profit Impact	Medium	Neutral	High	Neutral	Low	Low	High	High
Cost	Medium	High	Neutral	Low	High	High	Medium	Low
Payback	18 months	36 months	6 months	18 months	48 months	3 months	6 months	Immediate
Complexity	Low	High	Medium	Low	Low	High	Medium	Medium
Likelihood of Success	High	Medium	Low	Medium	Medium	Low	High	Medium

Figure 18.1 Operating Plan Initiative Matrix

and have the opportunity to add, you can do so with virtually no cost to the organization while likely lifting morale along the way.

Too many leaders early in their career believe aspiration and enthusiasm can increase capacity. The best leaders know how to set the proper speed limit. It's why organizations that focus properly always outperform their peers. Warren Buffet once said: "The difference between successful people and *really* successful people is that *really* successful people say 'no' to almost everything."[4]

Seek and Take Advice

Using subskills from Part III (Willingness to Seek and Take Advice), discuss your preliminary operating plan and key initiatives with your advisors. As you do so, consider a presentation that follows five elements:

- presentation of your baseline budget and the prior year's operating plan;
- explanation of key initiatives and how they will be measured;
- description of the most promising initiatives that you eliminated;
- a tactical plan for achieving the key initiatives;
- a rough budget that folds in the key initiatives with the baseline budget.

The purpose of the meeting is not to convince your advisors of your proposed operating plan. You're facilitating a conversation to cultivate ideation and creativity, which means that if your advisors do their job they'll come up with questions and challenges that you hadn't considered. You should find those welcoming.

Nonetheless, you're only human. Having noted their feedback and advice, initially do nothing. You'd made a substantial investment in time and energy into your key initiatives and in what will become your operating plan. If you immediately dig into their questions and challenges, you'll be susceptible to *confirmation bias*, finding ways to discount anything that is counter to your going-in position. To defend against that bias, put a few days distance between what you heard and processing their advice.

Once you decide on the key initiatives, after soliciting advice and considering any changes, fold those into your baseline budget, followed by a short tactical plan. The problem with long, detailed plans is they are never referred to during the year—becoming works of business art but not a tool for running your organization. Instead, find the equivalent of a 4x6 index card and put the essence of each manager's role in the operating plan on that card. Consider even putting the card with the key initiatives in a Lucite frame and placing it on each manager's desk. Every day they see what their role is in the operating plan and reinforce saying "no" to anything in the way.

The Power of 10

A few years after I joined the board of Asurion, they received a bid request that had the potential to transform the company. At the time, they had 150 employees and generated less than $25 million in revenue. With the bid request in hand, CEO Kevin Taweel asked his team, "What would it look like if we focused 10 times the energy than what might be considered normal?" His team thought he was exaggerating for effect. But Kevin meant his question literally. He wanted to harness the *power of 10* and see what would happen if they actually applied 10 times the effort. Asurion won the bid and set the company on a path to eventually reach billions in revenue.

The power of 10 remains in Asurion's arsenal, although they know to use it selectively—only in those cases where they identify an opportunity or problem that is so transformative, it is worth dropping virtually every other key initiative to focus on a single priority. When they do so, Kevin is always careful to take everything else off his team's plate. Otherwise, he's just asking people to work a little harder, for what will become lesser results—and that never works.

A Final Thought . . .

In the bestselling book *Switch,* Chip and Dan Heath suggest *scaling your bright spots* and to "find out what's working and do more of that."[5] If this advice seems exceedingly obvious, note that the book was on the *New York Times* Best Sellers List for 47 weeks. That's because most people naturally get it wrong. We commonly waste time racing after what's new and shiny—when what we should do is put more energy into what is already working. We disproportionately put energy into saving our troubled situations, or chasing an untested idea, while leaving our high-potential opportunities underserved.

While there are the rare legendary stories of leaders who refused to surrender a struggling idea, and then later it succeeded, in most cases that dogged behavior wastes time and diffuses your organization's focus. Typically, the easiest and fastest way to move forward is to do more of what is working: scaling your bright spots.

As you create your operating plan, use your baseline budget as the starting point to look for the wide-open doors that already exist. If your current plan is working, consider just running in the same direction, a little faster, for another year. There is wisdom in an operating plan that proposes nothing more original than continuing to scale your bright spots for as long as that keeps working.

The Operating Plan

1. Prioritization is a willingness to say "no" to attractive ideas, aware that by doing so you will probably never get to them.

2. An operating plan is not a budget, but an articulation of the goals and priorities for the coming year, metrics to measure progress, and a roadmap on how to get from here to there.

3. Begin by generating a *baseline budget*, which represents what the team believes will occur without implementing any new initiatives.

4. Convene your team to brainstorm initiatives for the following year, maximizing *ideation* and *creativity*.

5. Eliminate those initiatives with limited promise and develop the remaining initiatives with enough tactical detail to get a sense of the effort involved and the approximate cost.

6. Cross almost everything off the list.

7. Seek and take advice. Don't sell your advisors on your plan; get their unbiased guidance.

8. Use the *power of 10* where you identify a problem or opportunity that is worth dropping virtually every other project.

9. *Scale your bright spots.* The easiest and fastest way to move forward is doing more of what is working, doing the same thing and simply driving faster in the same direction.

19 Alignment Through Compensation

If you pick the right people and give them the opportunity to spread their wings, and then put compensation as a carrier behind it, you almost don't have to manage them.

—Jack Welch, former chairman and CEO of General Electric

When my son-in-law took a new job, he didn't receive a compensation increase—in fact, his commission upside dropped from 50% to 20%. Even though he'd worked for two large software companies and always finished at the top of his cohort, he decided to try a smaller, fast-growing firm. Conventional wisdom would think that he'd be working less hard in his new position—after all, isn't that how incentive compensation works?

But typical of star employees, my son-in-law's motivation to work hard never came from his employer dangling money in front of him. When former Stanford faculty member Jim Collins launched the team of researchers that led to the book *Good to Great*, the researchers collected a mind-bending 384 megabytes of data. Among their conclusions was the revelation that economic gains from compensation plans were *not* a factor in driving behavior:

> *We expected to find that changes in incentive systems, especially executive incentives, would be highly correlated with making the leap from good to great . . . [but] we found no systematic pattern.*
>
> *If you have the right executives on the bus, they will do everything within their power to build a great company, not because of what they will "get" for it, but because they simply cannot imagine settling for anything less.*

This discovery flew in the face of the orthodox notion that we can increase labor output through financial rewards. That antiquated belief assumes that good people hold back a portion of their energies until they receive more money. But if you employ the concepts from Part I of this book (Commitment to Building a Team), you already have a fantastic group in place. They are not going to work harder because you entice them with more money.

A company's performance is instead the result of a skilled and motivated team working in harmony. People are complex. They are influenced more by how they are regarded, whether they find the work interesting, their attitude toward their company and their boss, and being on a winning team. A survey by the firm Hays Specialist Recruitment found that 71% of all participants reported they would accept a lower paying job for the right benefits, culture, and career growth opportunities.[1] While some households don't have the luxury of taking a lower wage, the data show that most people will trade some compensation for the job they prefer.

This means that variable compensation matters, but not because you can make a good team member work harder through economic rewards. Employees want to know what is expected of them, clarity on how it will be measured, and recognition when a job is well done. Great leaders treat variable compensation as an institutionalized process that addresses these desires. Properly designed, variable compensation is a powerful tool in your efforts to get your team to set and adhere to priorities.

Variable Compensation

There are three principal types of compensation: *base compensation, benefits,* and *variable compensation.* Understanding how these work together allows you to strategically design a compensation program that aligns your team with your priorities.

Base compensation and benefits are predictable—your salary and health plan are known to you. Because of this, base compensation allows employees to build a household budget and save for future expenses (e.g., college and a house down payment). Benefits are also predictable, but unlike salary, your employees may value them differently. A health plan costing the company $10,000 per year may be worth more to employees who intend to start a family than to employees who are covered by their spouse's health plan. First-class airfares may be valued by some, while others might willingly fly coach in return for more base salary.

As you design your benefits, beware of trying to be all things to all people. You don't need to corner the entire labor market; you just need to fill your open positions. Excel at a few things that will differentiate you with a large enough pool of workers to meet your company's hiring needs, rather than having a me-too strategy that is unexciting to anyone.

Before considering any variable compensation, you need to first provide enough base compensation and benefits to satisfy your team's requirements for security. Creating economic stress and anxiety in the hope that you'll motivate people to work harder almost never increases performance.

Variable compensation provides clear direction on where you want folks to focus their efforts, followed by a mechanism to recognize success and provide a reward system. It's a powerful tool in your efforts to set and adhere to priorities. This begins by not using variable compensation as a source of financing, allowing you to adjust your expenses up or down based on how well the company did that year. This sometimes comes in the form of profit sharing or a year-end bonus based on overall profits. Doing so results in a system that attracts mediocrity and repels excellence because a program that rewards everyone in the same way means that lower performers are brought up, and the high performers are brought down—that's how averages work.

Generalized profit sharing also does nothing to reinforce the priorities assigned to individual team members.

Who you include in variable compensation should not be a function of seniority or a way to convey status. Look instead to members of your team who have a direct role in achieving your key performance indicators (KPIs) and the success of the operating plan. If the company's success depends upon a 10-Minute Turn, providing a bonus to the chief financial officer may be less impactful than providing a bonus to the team responsible for getting the peanuts on the plane.

Compensation, KPIs, and the Operating Plan

The variable compensation plan should be tied directly to your KPIs and operating plan and be used as a means to focus and reward the team's ability to hit those targets. As you make the team aware of your operating plan and KPIs, reinforce your priorities by focusing your variable compensation plan on those targets. It's the difference between recognizing and compensating for an individual's role in a successful 10-Minute Turn versus sharing in the results of the last quarterly earnings report.

Since your organization can only focus on just a few KPIs or priorities at a time, avoid the trap of "spray and pray," where you list so many elements that none have any importance. The best variable compensation plans have between one and four measurements, all consistent with the operating plan and each material to the final payout.

SMART Goals

Peter Drucker in his book *The Practice of Management*[2] popularized the mnemonic SMART, which stands for:

- Specific
- Measurable
- Attainable
- Relevant
- Time-Bound

Specific and Measurable

It's hard to hit a target if you don't know where to aim. If you tell a manager that their bonus is based on "getting collections in line," without determining the *specific* definition of what that looks like, and how you plan to *measure* it, don't expect success. To improve your collections and create alignment, you'll need to create goals that are specific and measurable.

The primary impediment to *specific* and *measurable* is rushing and cutting corners. Setting a goal of "reducing the over 90-day balance to $40,000 by the end of March" requires more effort on your part than "getting collections in line," but has a vastly higher chance of success. The same is true for those priorities that are not easily reduced to numeric targets. Without specific and measurable goals, the chances of success are also low. Non-numeric goals can also be specific and measurable—they just require more effort on your part.

Let's return to the example from Chapter 12 (Delegating), where we assigned this task:

> *We'll need to project square footage, by type (office, warehouse, vehicle storage), and drivetimes to our key customers' locations in 20-minute geo-fences, which you can do with Geotech's mapping software.*

Using the concepts of specific and measurable, increase the chances of success by adding the elements of specific and measurable into their variable compensation:

> *Twenty-five percent of your first-quarter bonus will be tied to determining whether we should renew the lease or move locations. I'll be looking for a report that has the following elements: (i) required square footage by department; (ii) three alternative locations that are available for lease; (iii) a drivetime map . . .*

Clearly this requires additional initial effort on your part. However, by tying your variable compensation plan to this delegated task, you've created clear specificity, and for both of you a method to measure success.

Attainable and Relevant

Your best players need to feel that achieving the plan is within their capabilities. Dangling financial incentives in the hopes that people will work harder would be an easy way to manage an organization, but it doesn't work that way. As my colleague, Jeffrey Pfeffer, professor at Stanford, writes, "There are, unfortunately, few shortcuts in leadership—and using financial incentives to fix companies isn't one of them."[3] To add structure to the concept of *attainable*, use these two easy concepts.

First, begin by setting your goals such that there is an 80% probability that your manager can achieve the base plan. Then, using a sliding scale for calculating the bonus, eliminate a winner-take-all outcome by creating a sliding scale. This allows you to provide an 80% probability of hitting the base target, while keeping in place a mechanism to reward outsized results and widening the results of what may be considered attainable.

For example, let's assume the plan addresses how many of your customers are retained from quarter to quarter. Your operating plan targets 94% each period, so your manager's incentive compensation might begin with this 94% customer retention. But it also provides for additional recognition up to 96% retention. As well, they will still earn some bonus if the target is missed slightly (Figure 19.1).

	Percentage Achieved				
	0%	25%	50%	75%	100%
Customer Retention Target	92%	93%	94%	95%	96%
Bonus Amount	$ -	$1,250	$2,500	$3,750	$5,000

Figure 19.1 Example Bonus Plan

The second element of an attainable plan is to maximize what is within the employee's control. When I rolled out a bonus plan for my first chief financial officer, his bonus included meeting the expense budget for his department. But his budget included expenses for which he had no control, such as rent (which was fixed in the lease) and insurance (which was a function of the total number of employees). In his incentive plan, I subtracted out these items and presented him with a structure that measured performance against this adjusted budget, which was more within his control.

Time-Bound

Bonuses should be paid no less frequently than quarterly. Any less frequent is too abstract and distant to be effective. Annual bonuses also delay recognition for accomplishments that happened early in the year. For instance, if you asked a manager to put in place an inside sales team in the first quarter of the year, under an annual plan you'd be withholding recognition of that work for nine months. Additionally, for elements of the plan that are subjective, measuring performance quarterly avoids the recency bias that leads us to overweight events later in the year, likely penalizing someone who crushed it in the first quarter and overly rewarding someone who finished strong.

Annual plans also lower the sense of urgency, as the reward is too disconnected from the performance. Recognizing the success of a project or initiative six months later is wasting the nonmonetary aspects of the program. An annual bonus also does not account for the normal ups and downs throughout the year. If a person stumbled big in the first half of the year, under an annual plan, no matter how well they perform in the second half, they won't see any reward, whereas if the plan resets every quarter, they get a fresh start. Finally, quarterly systems create four times the opportunities to reward and provide feedback, consistent with instant performance feedback.

Qualitative Targets: The 90-Day Plan

An operating plan often involves work that is critical to the long-term success of the company but doesn't lead to immediate financial results or straightforward numerical measurements. For example, the benefit of a new commission plan wouldn't show up straightaway in new sales, yet it might be central to the long-term success of the organization. The solution is to include qualitative targets in the form of a *90-day plan*.

The 90-day plan should have the same elements of SMART. For instance, you might specify that the commission plan includes how to transition the current salesforce to the new plan, along with implications for recruiting talent and addressing any employee turnover. You'll want to flesh out these details and milestones, many of which will be co-created. Breaking it down into steps such as these also helps you more accurately measure how realistic the overall goal is—an exercise in itself of achieving the concept of *attainable*.

Since your job is to help them hit their 90-day plan, not to stand back and see how they do, you'll include milestones. For instance, if the operating plan called for designing a new commission system in the first calendar quarter, include an interim step to deliver a draft of the commission plan midway in the quarter so you can see if they are on track and help them make any necessary corrections in time to achieve their 90-day plan. Remember, the goal is not to see if they succeed, but to make sure they succeed.

I found institutionalizing the subjective aspects of my operating plan into their variable compensation also helped me stick to my organization's priorities. The temptation to add new tasks to someone's plate, which come at the expense of the carefully prioritized operating plan, are enormous. By creating a written 90-day plan that ties into the operating plan, I was less tempted to load more tasks onto my team's plate throughout the quarter. The requirement to be SMART forced me to do a complete job of describing what was expected.

Pay Graciously

Make it clear that you want your team to succeed at earning the highest possible bonus. Begin by paying out bonuses soon after they are earned. When valued team members hit their targets, don't indicate a lack of enthusiasm for their work by deprioritizing the administrative work of processing the payment. Signal your enthusiasm by putting a check in their hand a few days following the last day of the quarter.

If your payroll system allows, instead of burying the bonus in their regular payroll, hand them a paper check with the incremental payment. Deliver it personally if possible, along with a thank you and some thoughts on the job well done. Because I wanted to match the bonus to what appeared on the check, I grossed up the net amount to offset taxes and withholdings. For instance, if someone's bonus was $1,000, instead of a lesser amount that would have been reduced for taxes and social security, I increased their bonus amount such that the *after-tax* amount was $1,000. There's a motivational difference between seeing the full $1,000 bonus in your hand, and getting an after-tax check for $879.63.

Lastly, where it applies, consider adding social events to your variable compensation tool chest. In my companies, I called this program *night-on-the-town,*[4] and would arrange for the employee to have a "date night" paid by the company. Because they often were uncertain how much to spend, I always made clear that we wanted them to splurge:

> *Peggy, I could not be happier to give you this bonus. I hope you and your husband celebrate your great quarter, which is why I left a credit at Ben Robert's Steak House. You both deserve to celebrate your hard work, and I want to see dessert and drinks on the bill—and include the cost of the sitter. The night-on-the-town is on me.*

A night-on-the-town not only showed appreciation, but hosting team members to dinner with their partners offered some pageantry and left both of them feeling positive about the company throughout the evening.

Transition from Legacy Plans

Compensation is sensitive to everyone, which is why changes need to be treated with care, compassion, and patience. As you transition to a new plan, never lose sight that your employees have bills to pay, vacations to plan, and college to save for. Creating uncertainty in their household budgets is counterproductive to aligning them with your organization's priorities. Anxiety is not a motivating emotion.

Roll out transitions and changes to their compensation gradually, probably by beginning just with your direct reports. Your aim is to create confidence in the integrity of the plan and comfort with the mechanics, and to work out any kinks before you extend the program to the next level within your team.

You may guarantee a minimum bonus for the first few quarters, providing only upside as they observe and experience how the new system works. This saves them from the unease that comes with paycheck uncertainty, and since your bonus plan is to help you set and adhere to priorities, you'll accomplish much of your goals even if the first few quarters are a trial run that includes a guaranteed payout.

If you don't have a bonus system in place or the level of bonus as a percentage of base salary is lower than you would like, rather than lower anyone's base salary and replace it with a bonus, roll future salary increases into the variable amount. For instance, let's assume someone is paid an annual base salary of $75,000 with no variable compensation. You'd like to have 15% of their target compensation as variable ($63,750 base, plus $11,250 bonus, to total $75,000). Instead of reducing their base salary, begin with a lower bonus potential of $5,000 that is in addition to their base salary of $75,000. In the next year, instead of an expected increase to their base salary, put that increase into their bonus potential. Over a few years you'll have them at 15% variable compensation without ever lowering their base salary, all the while accomplishing the goals outlined in this chapter.

A Final Thought . . .

My Stanford colleague Hayagreeva ("Huggy") Rao told me once that accountability is not a list of metrics, but a feeling of psychological ownership.[5] I took Huggy's advice to heart when I was a chief executive officer and kept a stack of crisp 50- and 100-dollar bills in my desk. If I observed or heard about an exceptional achievement, for example saving an upset customer, I would hand the employee one of those bills as a "sudden bonus."[6] I liked this method because I suspected that they wouldn't spend it right away, so that every time they reached into their bag or wallet, they'd see a reminder of what they'd accomplished and my appreciation. I set a culture that also recognized managers who alerted me to sudden bonus opportunities. I wanted my leadership team to have their eyes and ears on the lookout for opportunities to reward and recognize their team members.

A sudden bonus program can also be fun. My first company was in Texas, and I had a cowboy boot outfitted with a silver spur. At the monthly operating meeting, the boot sat in the middle of the conference table with envelopes inside for every member of a department, containing a cash bonus or other form of sudden bonus such as tickets to the rodeo or state fair. Each month, the whole company was anxious to learn which department "got the boot." At the end of the meeting, with some good-humored drama, I'd scoot the boot across the table to one of the managers. They'd hand out the envelopes to their team, and the boot would proudly stay in that manager's office until the next month, as a traveling trophy.

Alignment Through Compensation

1. Use variable compensation to communicate your priorities, center your team's attention, actively measure results, and provide regular feedback and coaching opportunities.

2. Base the metrics of your variable compensation on your operating plan and your KPIs, not the overall financial results of the company.

3. Use SMART as a guide to properly design a variable compensation plan:
   a. **Specific** and **Measurable:** It's hard to hit a target if you don't know where to aim.
   b. **Attainable** and **Relevant:** Your team needs to know that achieving the plan is within their capabilities.
   c. **Time-Bound:** Pay your bonuses no less than quarterly, creating more opportunities to acknowledge success, provide feedback, and maintain a sense of urgency.

4. Create a 90-day plan for qualitative targets, remembering to use SMART.

5. Pay graciously, quickly, and in person.

6. Take Huggy's challenge: use a "sudden bonus" to show appreciation, focus on your priorities, and create excitement.

7. Use economic gains from bonus plans not to drive behavior, but as a way to align your team around common objectives and to reward success.

PART V
An Obsession with Quality

20 Quality Drives Profit

We don't want to push our ideas on to customers, we simply want to make what they want.

—Laura Ashley

It wasn't my competition, higher expenses, or the Texas energy recession that almost cost me my first company—it was lousy service. I was 29 years old and with some investor money had bought a third-generation business from the original family. It was a storied company, and prior to my involvement, the customer base had been so loyal that the average client had been with them for 11.4 years—a number I'll never forget.

With my MBA learning, I knew profits came from increasing revenue and decreasing costs. The faster the technicians worked, and the more salespeople we hired, the more money we'd make. So that's what I did. I increased the number of salespeople by a third and told them to go sell what they could, as fast as they could. I pushed our field employees to get the work done in less time. I cut overtime and put monitors on the trucks to reduce fuel expense. We switched to a cheaper health plan to save money.

For six months profits increased, just like my professors said would happen. Then the ground shifted beneath me. I learned that a customer was leaving after 23 years with the company. A service manager left to work for the competition—something I was told had never happened in the 88 years the family owned the company. Morale was plummeting. More of the best people were leaving, and the closing rate on our sales proposals began to drop because the competition was spreading the word about our troubles.

Later than I should have, I got out from behind my desk, went into the field, and talked to customers to find out what was happening. Bill Gates famously said, "Your most unhappy customers are your greatest source of learning,"[1] and boy was that true in my case. I was embarrassed at what I saw and heard. When I called an advisor and told them the situation, he wisely suggested I read *Moments of Truth*, by Jan Carlzon, the former CEO of Scandinavian Airlines.

Moments of Truth

When Carlzon took over in 1981, he'd inherited one of the worst airlines in Europe. Like me, Carlzon wanted profits to increase, but unlike me, he understood that the easiest and most sustainable way to make more money was to create an outstanding customer experience. To get there, Carlzon didn't rely on slogans, marketing, or rallies. His approach to quality was tactical. He found out what mattered to his customers, then made operational changes to meet those requirements. He built systems to track on-time performance and pushed decision-making to the frontline. He created a new way of doing business that was not about talk, but about systems to support how his customers defined quality.

I came to appreciate that my MBA training had missed one of the most critical aspects of making money. Quality impacts profit more than any single operational area of a company. Quality positively impacts sales, pricing, and expenses. Three years after Carlzon took over, Scandinavian Airlines was the most punctual carrier in Europe. It would be twice awarded Airline of the Year. And did they make money. When he took over, they were losing 80 million Swedish kroner each year. Three years later they *made* 800 million kroner. Carlzon's book, and his philosophy, changed forever how I thought about making money.

Quality Drives Sales

Quality not only drives sales, but it's also the cheapest and easiest way to do so. Data supports this. Bain & Company found that companies that excel in customer experience increased revenues 4% to 8% faster than their competition.[2]

The reason begins with understanding the four ways to increase revenue, which I learned from Richard Reece. When Richard joined Iron Mountain as CEO, they had 70 employees and $3 million in revenue. When he retired, 17,000 employees generated more than $3 billion in sales. I was fortunate to serve on a board of directors with him, and one day he pulled out a black pen and drew a two-by-two matrix for me (Figure 20.1):

Figure 20.1 The Ansoff Matrix

A graduate of Clemson University, Richard speaks with a resounding Southern accent that halts others in mid-sentence. Using the Ansoff matrix, Richard explained that revenue from existing customers translates into higher profits because repeat customers stay longer, buy more, and more actively promote the company to others. New customers, on the other hand, require convincing to get them to leave their current relationships.

I later verified that new customers are six to seven times more expensive to attract than keeping an existing customer.[3] Richard's point was that in a world of limited time and resources, a company should first maximize the revenue it gets from those with whom it already does business, preferably by selling them products that the company already knows how to make.

Of course, to build a big company, you'll eventually need to know how to bring in new customers and create new products. After all, Richard's company ended up serving a quarter of a million customers in 58 countries. His argument, though, is that you should first take care of your current customers with the products and services you already provide, *before* expanding into new products with new customers—for the simple reason that it's easier, faster, and cheaper.

But if you want more of your existing customers' business, the price of poker is providing a quality customer experience. Once someone experiences your product or service, all the sales and marketing prowess won't get them to buy from you again if you disappointed them. Your existing customers already know what it's like to buy from you. If they're happy, it'll be easy to sell them more, and if not . . . best of luck.

All of which is critical because while people will buy more from you if they like their experience, 59% of buyers are extremely willing, or very willing, to switch providers based on a bad customer experience.[4] Frankly, I wonder why that share of buyers isn't 100%. When quality suffers, and your competition wants to take away your customers, it becomes very hard to convince them to buy more of your existing product or try one of your new products.

But too often managers try to drive sales by cranking up their sales force, unaware that increasing and maintaining quality is an easier, faster, and cheaper way. I've been directly involved in the purchase or management of more than 100 small to midsized businesses. In almost every case, new salespeople were hired, the website improved, and marketing investments were made. In every case, driving revenue through these methods fell short of expectations. It turns out that a great sales engine can't sell a mediocre product. Fantastic salespeople may help get you in the door or make an initial sale, but no amount of marketing or selling can cast off the anchor of an unexceptional product or service.

I'm not suggesting that sales and marketing is of no value. The exciting aspect of quality is that it sets up an interesting "virtuous cycle" with your sales and marketing organization. You get to have your cake and eat it to. Great salespeople gravitate to the companies selling the best quality products or services because they want to work for companies where they'll make more money, and they know they can sell more of a higher quality product. Which means companies selling quality goods end up with the best sales and marketing people—creating a further acceleration in sales growth.

Quality Drives Pricing

Pricing power is the next link between quality and profitability. Customers will pay 17% more to do business with a firm that has a high-quality product.[5] If what you sell is inferior, the opposite is true: The only way to get someone to buy a lesser quality good is to lower your price—generally by a lot.

Meanwhile, there is no greater single leverage point for profit than pricing. Increases (and decreases) go straight to the bottom line because the cost of goods is the same whether the price goes up or down. With a typical business, a price increase of only 5% may raise profits by 50% (Figure 20.2).

There is another interaction between quality and price. Customers expect that a higher-priced product generally has higher quality—one more "virtuous cycle." Let me explain with an example. When Glaxo came out with the heartburn drug Zantac as a competitor to SmithKline Beecham's Tagamet, instead of pricing Zantac based on what their competitor charged, Glaxo charged 50% *more* than Tagamet.[6] They knew Zantac had advantages, such as how often it needed to be taken, and that it had fewer side effects. Glaxo wanted to signal their quality differential to buyers by charging a higher price,[7] which they could only do if the product was better. It worked. Zantac was more profitable by charging a higher price, and Glaxo clobbered Tagamet in the marketplace because the higher price left customers assuming Zantac to be the better alternative.

	Base	5% Price Increase
Revenue	5,000,000	5,250,000
Cost of Goods	3,000,000	3,000,000
Admin Expense	1,500,000	1,500,000
Profit	500,000	750,000

Figure 20.2 Impact of Pricing

Quality Reduces Cost

In 1980, Philip Crosby published the book *Quality Is Free*, and he is often credited with that same phrase. But he learned the expression from his old boss at ITT, the famous industrialist, Harold Geneen. The saying came about when they were discussing a particular issue at one of their operations. There Geneen said, "I don't understand why they fight quality. It's free."

Geneen and Crosby later explained to the broader business community that quality is not the maximum number of features or services that can be imagined—because customers won't pay for features that they don't value. Quality is conformance to carefully thought-out customer requirements. If you engineer or design a product or service to perform in a certain way, and you understand that customers are willing to pay for those features, then the cost of those features is built into the pricing.

The true cost of quality is the *difference* between what it takes to make a great product and the direct costs associated with making a mediocre product. For instance, the internal cost of poor quality may be a repair that is covered under the product warranty or in fixing a software bug. External costs of quality include lost customers, product returns, and reputational damage. Quality is free because in most cases the added cost of good quality is offset by a reduction in the cost of poor quality.

People generally thought only of the expense associated with good quality, forgetting to consider the offsetting expense of poor quality. Crosby took what his boss said to him and created a framework that became a standard for how the best leaders understand quality (Figure 20.3).[8]

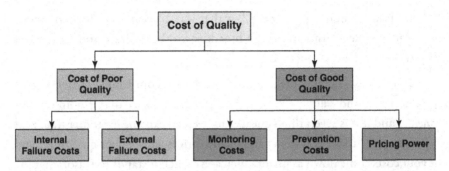

Figure 20.3 The Cost of Quality

Managers underestimate the cost of bad quality because only 15% of the cost of poor quality is easily observed and quantified. The quality expert Taiichi Ohno of Toyota Motor Corporation said, "Whatever an executive thinks the losses of poor quality are, they are actually six times greater."[9] Costs such as rework, defects, warranty, and returns may be known and measured, but the greater expenses such as lost sales, accidents, past due receivables, employee turnover, and rushed delivery are harder to identify.

In my own situation, we experienced the savings Ohno describes. After reading Carlzon's book, we instituted our quality improvements and stopped needing to send technicians back to customer locations to fix problems. We saw a marked reduction in customer attrition. Employee turnover dropped because while a daily dose of unhappy customers was tough on our team, once we became the highest quality provider, which we were, people wanted to come work for us. We used our quality as a recruiting weapon, getting our payback by taking back some of the best people from the competition. The costs we incurred to increase quality were far offset by these savings. By the time we sold the company to Citicorp Venture Capital four years later, we were measured as the most profitable company within our industry.

A Final Thought . . .

In today's world, where information shoots across the web instantly and broadly, an obsession with quality is even more important. A decade ago, 54% of people would repeat information about a bad customer experience to more than five people, while about the same number of people would tell others about a good experience.[10] But that was 10 years ago. Imagine today when that same sentiment can be broadcast to the entire world with a few keystrokes on Deets, Angie's List, or Yelp.

If the best salespeople want to work for companies with the best products . . . and selling to existing customers is easier than finding a new one . . . and if it is seven times cheaper to keep an existing customer than find a new one . . . and if you can charge higher prices with higher quality . . . and if your costs come down as quality increases—then it stands to reason that the easiest, fastest, and cheapest way to increase profit is *not* by hiring more salespeople, *not* by launching a marketing drive, and *not* by expanding into new markets or products, but by focusing on improving the quality of your existing product.

Quality Drives Profit

1. Quality increases sales. Repeat customers stay longer, buy more, and more actively promote the company to others.

2. Ansoff matrix: Drive revenue first by selling more of the same product or service to your existing customers. But to do so, you must provide a high-quality product or service.

3. A great salesperson can't sell a mediocre product.

4. The best salespeople want to work for companies with high-quality products.

5. Quality drives pricing power. There is no greater single leverage to profitability than with pricing, and there is no greater single leverage to higher pricing than quality.

6. Quality lowers cost. The true cost of quality is the difference between what it takes to make a great product and your direct costs associated with making a mediocre product.

21 Walk Behind the Tractor

Spend a lot of time talking to customers face-to-face. You'd be amazed how many companies don't listen to their customers.

—H. Ross Perot, founder, Electronic Data Systems

My father had a modest-sized business manufacturing farm equipment. He never sold anything directly to a farmer because like cars, farm equipment is sold through a dealer network. Growing up I never set one foot inside the offices of any of those dealers. Instead, on the weekend I'd walk the fields with my dad. With a tape recorder in his hand and walking behind a tractor, my dad would listen to the farmer describe how the harvester he'd bought performed in thick mud after a rain. The farmer was not the customer, but my dad understood the difference between the customer and the end user, and taught me the importance of *walking behind the tractor*.

Decades later, I cofounded what would become one of the nation's largest transporter of nonhazardous liquid waste. But along the way I forgot to *walk behind the tractor*. Most municipalities require restaurants to install traps to reduce the amount of oil and grease discharged into the public sewer system. Periodically those traps must be emptied, and we decided to get into that line of business.

For our existing business, we maintained a fleet of modern trucks that we kept clean and shiny. Our drivers wore fresh uniforms every day. We processed our own waste, so we had a cost advantage over the competition. We promoted those same features when we launched our grease trap service. The folks at the restaurant chain's headquarters liked our pitch, and we sold a lot of accounts. Business took off. Then the complaints started.

Cleaning a grease trap involves dragging a hose into a restaurant and operating a noisy pump. When the trap is opened the smell is awful. Yet we were requiring the drivers to meet with the restaurant managers, and to do so they had to arrive during business hours, the same time food was being prepared and customers were arriving. The restaurant managers didn't care that we were a few bucks cheaper or that our drivers were in uniform. Quality for them was showing up when the restaurant wasn't serving customers, and then getting in and out quickly and unnoticed. Our product turned out to be *lower* quality than our competitors because we had been using a definition of quality that had nothing to do with what the end user valued. I'd forgotten my father's lesson to 'walk behind the tractor'.

The Lake Wobegon Effect

The Lake Wobegon effect is a form of *confirmation bias* and is named after the NPR radio program that features the fictional town of Lake Wobegon. Each episode begins with a narrator's description of a town where "all the children are above average." The joke of course is that mathematically only half the children could be above average, while the other half had to be below average. When a 1981 study documented that a hilariously high 93% of American drivers rated themselves as "above average" drivers, this phenomenon came to be named the Lake Wobegon effect.[1]

The Lake Wobegon effect is reflected in how most company leaders rate their own product or service. Bain & Company found 80% of company leaders believed that they offered a superior customer experience. Well, it turns out that only 8% of their customers agreed with them![2] Which suggests that the odds are extraordinarily high that whatever quality assessment you have of your product or service is overblown.

Much of this misconception comes not from optimism or hubris, but from the more mundane result of on overreliance on data that are *available* and *familiar.* Take for example a healthcare company that I'd worked with for years. It used net promoter score (NPS)[3] as its exclusive measure of quality. NPS was developed in 2001 and is based on asking a single question of the respondent: "On a scale of 1–10, how likely are you to recommend this product or service?"

For the healthcare company, NPS was available and familiar, so much so that executive bonuses depended upon hitting NPS targets. The leadership team focused on NPS not because they had proof it was the best measure of quality (they did not), but because that's how it had always been done.

Customer satisfaction scores like NPS are used at 80% of customer service departments, even though data from the *Harvard Business Review* shows that it is a poor measure of whether your customers want to stay with you—only 28% of *unsatisfied* customers intended to leave their current supplier, yet 20% of *satisfied* customers also intended to find a new supplier.[4] This explains why, after the healthcare company rolled out improvements in the stability and quality of their software, vastly improving the product, their NPS score barely budged.

The second problem with most customer satisfaction scores is they almost always suffer from a "small n" problem and a *selection bias*—which together reflect the saying "garbage in, garbage out." I have sat in countless board meetings where an NPS is reported, only to find that the "n" was infinitesimal; only 3% of the customers they asked even responded. Hardly a large enough sample size to be trustworthy.

In defense, the case is sometimes made that a small response rate can accurately represent the sentiment of the entire cohort. But the data suffer from an additional problem: selection bias. Certain customers are more, or less, likely to respond to mass surveys. Think of it like this: when you get out of your rideshare and are asked to rate the driver on a five-star scale, does your *likelihood* of responding change depending upon whether the driver was incredibly friendly and the car was immaculate (5 stars), or if the service was just perfectly good (4 stars)? If you find yourself more likely to participate in surveys if you had a particularly good or bad experience, you now understand selection bias. Combine that with a small n, and you see the magnitude of the issue.

The next way we incorrectly measure how our customers feel is explained through a well-known tendency to rely on quality measurements that give us the answer we want: the *observer-expectancy effect* that I introduced in Chapter 1 (Hire for Outcomes). Let me explain through an example. I once asked a seasoned CEO how she measured quality in her company, and she told me that her leadership team relied upon online reviews, namely Yelp. I was surprised, given there is well-documented error with most online reviews, such that companies should never rely on them to gauge how well they are doing.[5] I looked up her scores on Yelp and wasn't surprised that Yelp was the company's preferred yardstick. Sixty-eight percent of its reviews were "excellent" and another 23% "very good."

The company's quality might have been that good, but that's not why management used them. They stuck to Yelp out of the observer-expectancy effect: rigging the experiment to get the desired outcome. In my friend's case, the whole company wanted to believe they were doing a great job, and so they unwittingly used the measurement that gave them that answer.

Stanford business professors David Larcker and Brian Tayan identified the final way bias impacts our estimation on what our customers think—an overreliance on our personal instincts.[6] I especially like their example of a large fast-food chain. The management of the restaurant chain had such a conviction that low employee turnover was the principal driver of customer satisfaction that they told the Stanford team not to bother looking elsewhere. Their entrenched belief was that when they reduced turnover, quality went up. When the research team asked them why they felt the connection was so strong, even though they had no supporting data, they told them, "We just *know* this is the key driver."

Nonetheless, the Stanford team wanted to find out for themselves. And it was a good thing, because it turned out that it was not overall employee turnover that mattered, but the turnover of only the store manager. This restaurant chain had spent years of energy and resources addressing quality by focusing on overall employee turnover when the key leverage point was to focus that energy into retaining just their managers.

None of these biases are deliberate attempts to fool ourselves—which is where the danger lies. Cognitive biases represent an *unconscious* miswiring of our thought processes. Just as you need to solve for confirmation bias in reference checking by doing them when you are choosing among candidates rather than confirming your selection, so too you need to create similar guardrails if you want to accurately understand how your customers feel about your product or service, which begins by following them home.

Follow Them Home

Scott Cook built Intuit into a company that makes $2 billion in operating profits each year by selling products such as TurboTax, QuickBooks, and Mailchimp. A critical aspect of Intuit's enduring success is Cook's practice that he calls "follow them home," his version of walking behind the tractor. As Cook describes:

> By observing our customers in their "natural habitat," we're able to glean what they like, what they don't like, what challenges they may encounter, and how they use the product.

Scott Cook didn't invent software, the internet, or the modern-day accounting system. But he was a patient, astute, and relentless observer of how customers interacted and used his products. Cook created a culture at Intuit of observing their products through the end user's experience. Based on how the customers use the product, follow them home allows Intuit to know what features to add, what to drop, and where to focus Intuit's energies. Intuit's chief financial officer credits "follow them home" as a principal reason Intuit dominates their markets:

> That process of observing the customers provides us with deep customer immersion and has helped us focus on the things customers really like, and appreciate, and not burden them with things you can do but nobody cares about.[7]

An NPS survey might give you a sense of your customer's overall satisfaction, but it won't do a lick of good showing you what you need to do to beat the competition next year. Intuit's story reminded me how, when Paul English was getting Kayak started, he took customer service calls for a half hour each day. I asked him whether that mindset was influenced by his time working at Intuit, and Paul told me, "Intuit influenced me massively with how I think about the customer. I give them—and Scott Cook, specifically—credit for this mindset."

Ignore what your team tells you. Cast aside your instincts and assumptions. Disregard the experiences of your friends. Don't talk to the folks at the company headquarters, and pay little heed to the latest marketing survey. If you want to stay ahead of the competition, you must follow your customers home and observe your product or service being used.

The Power of Verbatim

If Henry Ford had used SurveyMonkey to ask Americans whether they were satisfied with their current mode of transportation, we might still be riding horses because, as he famously said, people would have told him, "Give us faster horses."

It's now so easy to design a questionnaire and send it to thousands of potential respondents that we often replace the quaint act of talking to our customers with the comfort and convenience of electronic surveys. But we know that surveys suffer from a "small n," selection bias, and are generally dumbed down to a few generalized questions. They provide data for graphics and presentations, but little in the way of insight.

Tom Feeney is my champion for the *power of verbatim*. Safelite Autoglass is a 75-year-old company in the mundane business of replacing broken windshields. Feeney had been with Safelite for 20 years before being promoted to CEO, and prior to his promotion had led the company's retail operations, global sales and support, and was its chief client officer. I list those positions to demonstrate how remarkable it was that after 20 years at Safelight, principally in customer-facing roles, when he became CEO, he set aside his own opinions and had his teams speak directly to his end users:

> We decided to stop worrying about the numerical NPS and instead pay attention to what the customer's verbatim [comments] told us . . . This is a fuller, more textured way to be looking at our business through our customers' eyes.[8]

While Scott Cook watches customers use his product, Feeney chats with them about what they want and need. In this way his team learned, for example, that one of his customer's critical wants was quick and simple ease of ordering. That led Safelite Autoglass to redesign its user-interface, reducing the number of clicks required to schedule a job from 40 to 15. The company also learned that its customers wanted to track the technician's physical status while they waited, not just their expected arrival time. This led to the development of a feature similar to a ride sharing app that shows the live location of the technician. None of this could have been learned in a survey because no one would have thought to ask, "Would you like to track the technician's physical status on your phone: yes or no?" The idea had to first come from listening to his customers, verbatim.

Safelite Autoglass has been around for nearly eight decades in the prosaic work of replacing chipped windshields. Yet by applying the power of verbatim, Feeney doubled sales in less than 10 years. The lesson from Feeney, English, and Cook is that understanding what matters to various customer segments is not about surveys, but by your team getting out from behind their desks, following your customers home, and listening to them verbatim.

Predictive and Diagnostic Measurements

Having followed the end users home and heard from them verbatim, you're creating a definition of quality that allows you to find a place in the market where you can succeed. But having defined quality, you'll now need to understand how to use *predictive* and *diagnostic* tools.

Most quality scores simply *measure* what has already happened. Predictive tools allow you to *manage* the outcome. The difference is enormous. Imagine you own a chain of donut stores. The segment of the market you're chasing values two features: how quickly your customers get in and out, and whether their favorite donut is in stock. With this information, you develop two key performance indicators (KPIs):

- maximum wait time in line;
- occurrences a requested donut was out of stock.

Using concepts from Chapter 17 (Key Performance Indicators), you know that if you get these two inputs right, the outcome will be a happy customer. Therein lies the distinction. Instead of finding out whether you have happy customers (measuring the past), by using a predictive tool you *create* happy customers.

Predictive measurements are powerful because they are operationally actionable and impact the future. For example, if your tools notify you that more than three customers are in line, you can manage the outcome by adding another person to the shift before the line gets any longer, thereby creating happy customers. With systems in place to monitor when you're close to running out of cinnamon twists, you'll start baking more *before* you run out.

Diagnostic measurements are used in conjunction with predictive measurements. They collect after-the-fact data that allow you investigate what you need to do operationally to reinforce what's working or repair what's broken. Too often they are misused only to keep score, but used correctly, diagnostic tools begin a process of explaining why something happened, so you can manage the outcome. The four most common diagnostic tools are NPS,[9] customer effort score (CES),[10] first contact resolution (FCR),[11] and customer satisfaction (CSAT).[12]

Returning to our donut store, imagine you've been managing against the two previously described KPIs, which were your predictive measurements. As a result, the cinnamon twists are always in stock, and the line is generally short. But let's say you also collect diagnostic information, which you do by using a mobile device that you rotate among your donut shops (Figure 21.1).

Figure 21.1 Diagnostic Measurement

You won't know why a customer presses a smiling face or a frown; all you know is whether they did or not. But if your predictive KPIs are correct, you would expect to see a correlation between your diagnostic measurements and the predictive measurements (Figure 21.2). Put another way, the store with the shortest wait time and fewest stock-outs of cinnamon twists should get the most "happy face" presses. If this proves to be true, you're probably on the right track and should keep executing against your operational plan.

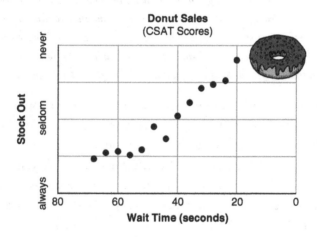

Figure 21.2 Diagnostic and Predictive Correlation

But what if the happiest customers do not correspond with your predictive scores? Based on the diagnostic measurement, you don't know why the store with the shortest wait time and the one that never runs out of cinnamon twists had more than the expected frowns, but it will have identified that you have a problem that requires some time behind the tractor.

What you subsequently learn in these verbatim conversations is that your customers are happy with the length of the line and the cinnamon twists are still a hit. The issue is that you discontinued the iced coffee a month earlier, and they ain't happy about that. But because you used a diagnostic measurement in conjunction with your predictive measurement, you have time to make the adjustments *before* very many of your customers switch to buying their morning coffee from your arch rival across the street.

A Final Thought . . .

Using quality as a weapon against your competitive rivals is not an exercise in intuition or gut feel. It's not about genius. It is *not* the product of a brainstorm session among your management team. It's about collecting actionable data directly from your customers, and acting with tactical authority. As the quality experts Frédéric Debruyne and Andreas Dullweber put it:

> *Experienced leaders sift through early initiatives to identify those that work well, reinforce the vision, and deserve more resources, while avoiding or quickly ending initiatives that don't matter to most target customers. They form these insights by analyzing customer feedback combined with data from other market research, financial data, press reports, and social media listening posts.*[13]

An obsession with quality is not about slogans or aspirations. The obsession comes from a deliberate, data-based exercise involving testing ideas, tracking the results, and iterating until you understand the intersection of what matters to the customer and where you can win. And in companies ranging from everyday industries such as Safelight Autoglass to innovators like Intuit, the results of applying these quality *subskills* to your organization can be extraordinary.

Walk Behind the Tractor

1. Beware the *Lake Wobegon effect,* which causes leaders to exaggerate their impressions of their product quality. No one wants to believe they are providing a lousy service or product.

2. Relying on data that are readily *available* and *familiar* is the most common reason leaders incorrectly measure their customers' sentiment.

3. Avoid quality measurements that give you the answer you want: the *observer-expectancy effect.*

4. Beware the two common issues with most customer satisfaction measurements: the *small n* and *selection bias.*

5. *Follow them home*: A competitive weapon few of your rivals will bother to take advantage of.

6. *Power of verbatim*: Going beyond surveys and forms to gain insights and discoveries that your rivals will miss.

7. *Predictive measurements*: Tools that allow you to *manage* the outcome instead of after-the-fact measurements that tell you what already happened.

8. *Diagnostic measurements*: Tools used in conjunction with *predictive measurements* that collect data to investigate past events and influence future decisions.

9. Use data to drive quality. An obsession with quality results from a deliberate, data-based exercise involving testing ideas, tracking the results, and iterating until you understand the intersection of what matters to the customers and where you can win.

22　A Vow to Wow

Do what you do so well that they will want to see it again and bring their friends.

—Walt Disney

arvard's Michael Porter was first to point out that business is not a winner-take-all endeavor. In most industries, multiple competitors are succeeding in different markets. This explains how Toyota and Tesla have both won in the electric vehicle market. Each offer high-quality products and serve consumers who care about the carbon emissions. Yet they sell to customers who define quality differently. Both succeed by avoiding being all things to all customers.

Today the flow of information is close to instantaneous. Competitors can match your price with a keystroke, use social network platforms to hire away your stars, and source raw materials anywhere from Tennessee to Tasmania. Through remote work, upstarts can access a global workforce. Which means that today it's nearly impossible to craft a sustainable competitive advantage by competing head-to-head with everyone in the marketplace. Winning requires carefully identifying a customer segment that has unique definitions of quality and then meeting those needs with *a vow to wow*.

Find a Corner of the Market

This is where small and midsized companies have an enormous advantage. Let me explain, again with an example. Today, there is a small but flourishing

226

market for independent bookstores. After a contraction from the one-two-three punch of big box retailers like Barnes & Noble, the entrance of Amazon, and new ways to read such as the Kindle, independent booksellers were closing or going bankrupt—one right after another.

But since 2010, the number of indie bookstores has grown 50%.[1] Harvard business professor Ryan Raffaelli writes that indie bookstores have thrived because they have found their corner of the market, which he defines as community, curation, and convening.[2] These independent bookstores don't compete with Amazon on price, convenience, or availability. They are thriving because they seek customers who want something that Amazon or a Kindle can't offer. As the *Washington Post* reports, the growth in indie bookstores is fueled by "a connection with the community instead of fighting Amazon for every dime."[3]

The point is that there is not a single definition for quality, just like there is not a single definition of an electric car buyer or a book reader. Successful organizations use subskills to take an analytical approach to defining quality and then hunt to find a corner of the market that their competition has missed or is not interested in serving.

In the bestselling book *Moneyball*, Michael Lewis tells the story of how the Oakland A's found success by using analytics to find a unique market for players. In early 2000, they had a fraction of the financial resources available to teams such as the Boston Red Sox or New York Yankees. They couldn't compete for the same marquee players, and so Oakland's general manager, Billy Beane, investigated other ways to measure the quality of a player to find a market where he could recruit from a pool of overlooked players.

Beane and his team discovered that a player's on-base percentage—how frequently a batter made it to first base—was a better indicator of the batter's likelihood of generating runs than his batting average (the conventional metric for measuring an offensive player). By recruiting players with unique characteristics, instead of competing for the same players, they had a market of talent to themselves. After implementing this strategy, following years of poor results, the Oakland A's had their best season in a dozen years and went on to the playoffs.

In an interesting example from business, a UK-based bank applied the same concept to discover a profitable customer segment in banking, one that valued detecting, deterring, and fast resolution of fraud over all else.[4] In so doing, it used *Moneyball* concepts to find its own corner of the market. While other banks chased customers who measured quality by conventional measures such as the availability of ATM machines, this bank grabbed an underserved market by avoiding being all things to all customers, creating a service offering that mattered to a narrower definition of quality, and then dominating that particular market.[5]

Wowing Your Customers

Meeting the basic quality requirements of a customer is not enough to build loyalty. To build a moat around your customers, you'll need to *wow* them, and there is no better example on how to do that than with Tony Hsieh and Zappos.

At a time when everything from dog food to ready-to-prepare meals were being marketed, sold, and delivered to our front door via the internet, Zappos was founded with the unremarkable idea of selling shoes online. Yet, within a dozen years, Zappos would exceed a billion in revenue and become one of the top 10 companies to work for in the United States.[6] Zappos' success, and the moat Tony Hsieh built around his customers, resulted from a *vow to wow*.

Consider that today we can get from our living room couch to a seat on any airline without ever interacting with another person. Using just our phones, we can buy a ticket, request a rideshare, download a boarding pass, pass TSA security, and self-scan a QR code at the airline gate—never having to interact with a single person. The same is true with getting groceries to our front door or filling our car with gas.

These innovations in how we buy things have saved billions in labor expense and in many ways improved the customer experience. But as Hsieh noticed, they also removed many of the traditional opportunities organizations once had to build loyalty. If the Cheerios that were ordered off your phone and dropped off by DoorDash taste the same whether they were bought through Safeway or Albertsons, and you never directly interact with anyone during the process, how can a grocer provide a differentiated customer service experience that leads to a loyal customer?

In response to this, Hsieh could have pursued the strategy of dropping the cost of a pair of shoes from $92.00 to $89.00, attracting customers by saving them three bucks. A lot of companies did just that. But that's an advantage he knew any competitor could wipe out with a single keystroke—or as the expression goes, a "race to the bottom." What Hsieh wanted was, as Michael Porter describes, a sustainable competitive advantage.

Research shows that *wowing* results in five times more sales than paid advertising and is frequently less costly than paying for mostly unnoticed ads on social networks. Remarkably, even the people who earn their living proposing sales and marketing plans agree. Two-thirds of marketing professionals acknowledge that word-of-mouth marketing is a better way to drive your business than conventional marketing.[7]

But no one talks about a service experience that met expectations. For that to happen, you must wow your customer. If Zappos wanted to sell shoes over the internet, Hsieh understood that he had to find a different definition of quality—one that would appeal to a distinct segment of the market. And then wow them. He did so by going after customers who wanted a higher level of service than a website could provide, and then systematically and structurally providing a buying process that encouraged direct interaction between his customers and his team members.

While most companies save money by trying to get a computer to solve a customer's issue, Zappos tries to talk directly to their customers. Instead of sending customers to self-service options, saving labor expense, Zappos put its customer service phone number at the top of every page of its website and made it available on every package it sent. Hsieh understood that he couldn't wow anyone by handing them off to a computer—or as Zappos puts it:

Calling a company with an issue you need help with, and ending up talking to an automaton, is arguably one of the Worst. Things. Ever. Happily, Zappos customers never have to perish attempting to climb a phone tree to reach us—and a live human being generally answers all calls in less than one minute. Awesome, right? Everyone knows being on hold is for the birds.

What Hsieh did was to take that same three dollars and put it against being "maniacally obsessed with making sure our customers are happy." To Professor Porter's point, not to *all* shoe buyers, just the ones Zappos was after. Hsieh didn't try to serve buyers who defined quality as the lowest price. He went after those who wanted a personal customer experience—and it turned out to be a $2 billion corner of the market.

Service Recovery Paradox

Your customers know that soup sometimes arrives cold, deliveries are late, and new software releases often come with bugs. The *service recovery paradox* is the concept that loyalty is not earned by being perfect all the time. It is by proving how well you do when things go wrong. The data show that the most loyal customers are not those who have never had a problem, but those who have had a setback that the company resolved with unexpectedly great service— what came to be understood as the service recovery paradox (Figure 22.1).[8]

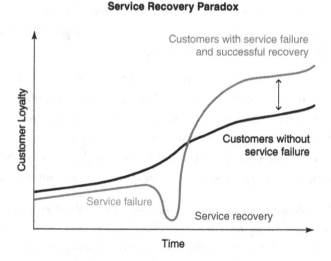

Figure 22.1 Service Recovery Paradox

The service recovery paradox begins with recognizing that no one talks positively about the time their soup arrived at the right temperature. They also generally don't talk negatively about the time the soup was cold but was routinely replaced with hot soup. What we do know, however, is that people talk about the time the soup arrived cold and the manager responded with an in-person apology and a complimentary dessert.

Which means that a disappointed customer is not a cost to incur, but an opportunity to create loyalty. For most organizations, this requires a gargantuan shift in culture and tactics. If your organization penalizes employees for mistakes, then those opportunities for the service recovery paradox are missed. For instance, if the server knows that reporting room temperature soup will result in an interrogation as to who messed up, then don't be shocked when the server quietly just gets the customer a new bowl of soup and moves on to the next table. The mishap goes unreported. No free dessert. No one was wowed.

When I read *Moments of Truth* in time before I ruined a three-generation family business, I came to understand the service recovery paradox. I institutionalized sensitive account alerts to promote reporting of missteps. The deal was simple. If someone reported a client issue using the sensitive account alert system, there were no ramifications to anyone. The sensitive account alert essentially became a get-out-of-jail-free card. The opposite was also true. If the company learned of a disappointed customer, and those involved failed to submit a sensitive account alert, there were consequences to those who failed to report the situation. We further institutionalized the program by assigning a manager whose only job was to promote the practice of submitting sensitive account alerts throughout the company, and then addressing the customer problems with the service recovery paradox in mind. Beyond the quality improvements, this program was perhaps the single most profitable decision we made at the company.

Quality as a Process (Three Ss)

Sam Walton understood that if he wanted to take customers from Target, K-Mart, and JCPenney, he needed to go beyond expectations. "The goal as a company is to have customer service that is not just the best," he once said, "but is legendary." Of course, the CEOs of his competitors also wanted to offer great service. The difference was not Sam Walton's aspiration, but the *scalable, sustainable,* and *simple* processes he created to fulfill those aspirations.

The mistake many leaders make is believing that quality is a "mindset" or that it can be achieved through a slogan like "Quality Is King!" An obsession for quality requires three Ss that combine to create sustainable, scalable, and simple processes. Your customers don't care what you say in your commercials; the only thing that matters to them is whether you have met their definition of quality. The only way to achieve that high quality over an extended period of time—consistently throughout your company—is to have quality built into your processes. For instance, instead of Walton telling his store managers to make customers feel welcome, he institutionalized greeters, a simple example of an operational tactic that was sustainable, scalable, and simple.[9]

Implementing three Ss begins with getting the product or service right the first time. The reason to get it right the first time is that your cost structure demands doing so—fixing a problem after the fact is very expensive. This is so true that the concept of Six Sigma, a concept whereby 99.73% of your product or service is right the first time, took off in the mid-1980s and allegedly saved GE over a billion dollars.[10] Quality is not a virtue. It is a cost-saving, revenue-generating strategy to succeed in the marketplace. An obsession with quality is so you can make more money.

The impact of the cost of poor quality at the point of delivery was captured in a remarkable survey of 1,300 companies across a wide spectrum of industries.[11] The research team examined the respondents' defect rates and then put the companies into five tiers, ranking best to worst. On average, each mistake took about two hours of employee time to correct. Using the mean wage rate across the surveyed companies, those in the top tier saved a walloping $13,400 per employee over those in the bottom tier.

In a telecommunications company I ran, we adopted 100% inspection of every customer installation, something unheard of in the industry. Initially many of the managers thought the idea too expensive, and tried to convince me that random inspections made more economic sense. But by then I'd come to appreciate that if the installation team understood there was a certainty that defects would be identified, they'd get it right the first time—put another way, that quality would be free. That's what happened. Our rework rate dropped to almost zero. The money we saved far offset the cost of inspection. Instead of holding town hall meetings, pitching the team on "going the extra mile," tacking posters up in the lunch room, or working with an outside agency to develop a slogan, we put our energy into a scalable and sustainable *process* for ensuring quality.

More About Simple

In achieving quality, complexity is your enemy. Most quality issues result from a variation from standard, and as complexity increases, the chances of variations grow at an exponential rate. To make my point, let's imagine we're together at the shooting range, learning to shoot.[12] We both fire 10 rounds at the target. Our instructor takes out her binoculars and announces that I got five shots in the bullseye while you got none. Based on that, we might assume I'm the better shot. But my boasting is short-lived when she retrieves the targets (Figure 22.2).

Who's the Better Shot?

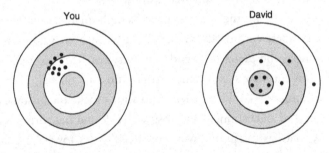

Figure 22.2 The Better Shot?

She tells us that you are the better shot. The reason of course is that your shooting is more consistent than mine. I may have managed more in the bullseye, but they happened through random deviations. For you, a slight adjustment to how you hold your cheek against the stock of the gun was all it took for you to get 8 for 10 in the bullseye on the next target.

When designing processes for quality, the more complexity you build into your systems, the greater the likelihood your shots will be all over the target. The more steps in your process, the more variations that can occur, which means the error rate increases.

For example, if you tell members of the call center to answer the phone politely, you're inviting a degree of variability into your system; each employee determines their own version of polite, and the manager must then monitor, evaluate, and give feedback on all these different versions. If, on the other hand, you tell them to always answer the phone with, *"It's a great day at Wind River Environmental, how can I help you?"* everyone says the same thing, the supervisor can easily monitor it, expectations are clear, and your chance of a sustainable and scalable process is vastly higher.[13] This concept becomes all the more critical the greater the intricacy of the product. For example, in software, the simplest code almost always has the fewest bugs. This was the genius of Sam Walton's greeter—it was not just scalable and sustainable, but pretty darn simple.

A Final Thought . . .

Amy Errett's company, Madison Reed, dominates the hair-coloring market for customers who want the convenience of a high-quality, at-home solution. They don't compete with products like Clairol, which are sold in drugstores, or for customers who prefer high-end salon services. Amy's company serves a customer segment that has a unique definition of quality, one that she identified as underserved. Like Hsieh, Amy didn't make the mistake of trying to be all things to all customers, but instead has found her corner—a corner, by the way, that has catapulted Madison Reed's sales toward a quarter of a billion dollars as of this writing.

It is a common mistake to chase every customer, and in so doing you impress no one. *Wowing* your target customer necessarily means that there will be those who love what you have to offer, and those who prefer to go elsewhere. If you chase every customer, you'll become operationally overwhelmed, and in the end mediocre at everything. Instead, think about quality the same way as Hsieh did when he created Zappos, or Amy with

Madison Reed—building an enduring company by finding a corner of the market that defines quality differently, and then satisfying your customers with a vow to wow.

A Vow to Wow

1. Remember that business is not a "winner-take-all" endeavor.

2. Use analytical *Moneyball* tactics, not instinct or guessing, to identify unique market niches that are ignored and to find where you can win.

3. To generate word-of-mouth buzz, you have to *exceed* customer expectations, not simply meet expectations.

4. Commit to a *vow to wow*, which results in five times more sales than paid advertising, distinguishes you from all the rest, and is far less expensive than traditional sales and marketing.

5. Cede certain markets to your competition. *Wowing* some customers necessarily means that there will be those who go elsewhere.

6. Take advantage of the *service recovery paradox*, exceptional correction of mistakes that can lead to deep customer loyalty.

7. Create systems, incentives, and processes (not slogans) to take advantage of the service recovery paradox.

IMPLEMENTING THE FIVE MUST-HAVE SKILLS FROM THE MANAGER'S HANDBOOK

Go out there and try to be good. If you go out there and try to be good, you've got a chance to be great.

—Rich Dubee, pitching coach

At the beginning of this book, I told you the story of Roy Halladay pitching a no-hitter and how his coach told him before the game, "Go out there and try to be good. If you go out there and try to be good, you've got a chance to be great." I wrote this book because I care about leadership. I also know that great leaders have the potential to do great things—and this world needs some of that right now. In so doing, you'll have a positive impact on people's lives—maybe even more than that. I'd like you to get your shot at being great. Which is why in our final moments together, I want to make the case that you should not pick and choose which among the *five skills* you'll now decide to implement.

In learning to play the piano, mastering both hands moving together is one of the most difficult steps—but if you don't do so, you'll never get past "Chopsticks." There are things in this book that are like that—harder and less appealing to implement than others. Just like you can't skip steps in learning the piano, there is no shortcut to great management. Organizing a team interview with structured questions is harder than breezing over the resume a few minutes before you meet the candidate. *Shallow work* is easier than *deep work*. So too is sending to your customers an online quality survey instead of using the *power of verbatim*. But if you want the chance to be great, you have to do the hard stuff, alongside the rest.

Despite starting over 50 years later, and in one of the oldest businesses ever, Sam Walton did circles around JCPenney, Target, and K-Mart. It wasn't because Walton invented the department store. It was because he hired better people, maintained his focus, listened to advice, managed his time carefully, and was obsessed with how his customers defined quality. Sam Walton may not have run his meetings in exactly the way this book suggests, but he did run effective meetings. Which is why you can't become the next Sam Walton unless you master these five skills and their subskills—which includes the ones you don't want to do.

It will be tempting to select which of these subskills to implement. If you do so, you'll most likely pick the easy ones and pass on those that are hard, tedious, boring, and unpopular with your team. As the billionaire venture capitalist Ben Horowitz says, this is the hard thing about hard things.

But there is a turbo-charging that happens when all five skills come together. Imagine the difference if, as you *walk behind the tractor*, you do so knowing how to *listen like Joe*. At your side is a remarkable team that you found through *hiring for outcomes* and taking care during the *100-day window*. You coached them using *Radical Candor* and *instant performance feedback*, and they don't leave to work for your competitor because you're alert to issues through *exit interviews* and *360° reviews*. When you come together in meetings, they are effective and purposeful, and you have a network of *advisors* to turn to when you have questions or doubts. Your team marches fast and in the same direction because you have a prioritized *operating plan* and a set of impactful *KPIs*.

If you want a chance at being great, you can't just implement the easy skills. To be great you must do them all. Even the hard ones.

Which is why, until the five skills become habit, I suggest you keep this book on your desk. Put it where you will see it every day. Make its physical presence a reminder of your commitment to implement the five skills learned from those managers who know how to get things done. Then push mastery of the subskills across all levels of your organization. A great orchestra requires more than a single pianist; it demands a team of skilled musicians. So too does your organization. Consider the power when your entire organization masters the five skills required to get things done. Leadership is about being the conductor, not the player.

Lastly, once your entire organization has implemented the five skills, give your worn-out copy of this book to someone you know who is outside your organization. Pay it forward, as the saying goes. When it becomes your turn to be the mentor, show the next generation of leaders that while they may already be good, they too deserve their chance to be great.

NOTES

Introduction

1. Collins, J. (2001). *First Who, Then What*.

Chapter 1

1. Collins, J. (2001). *Good to Great: Why Some Companies Make the Leap . . . and Other Don't*. New York, NY: Harper Business.
2. Leadership IQ, *Why New Hires Fail*, 2011 and 2020.
3. Cappelli, P. (2019, May–June). Your approach to hiring is all wrong. *Harvard Business Review*.
4. Gladwell, M. (2019). *Talking to Strangers*. New York, NY: Little, Brown and Company.
5. Adler, L. (2007). *Hire with Your Head: Using Performance-Based Hiring to Build Great Teams*. 3rd ed. Hoboken, NJ: Wiley.
6. Ibid.
7. Information demonstrating a history of compensation increases can be a strong indicator of success within the organization; however, some states and municipalities prevent organizations from asking about prior compensation to prevent salary discrimination against groups historically underpaid against other groups (for example, pay disparities between men and women). If you are permitted to ask prior compensation questions, have safeguards in place to make sure the information is not used to discriminate in your pay structure.

8. Smart, G., and Street, R. (2008). *Who.* New York, NY: Ballantine Books.

9. Adler, L. (2007). *Hire with Your Head: Using Performance-based Hiring to Build Great Teams.* 3rd ed. Hoboken, NJ: Wiley.

Chapter 2

1. The name has been changed to protect the privacy of the individual.

2. Martin, J. (2014, January 17). For senior managers, fit matters more than skill. *Harvard Business Review.*

3. Greenberg, A. (2015, January). Why employee onboarding matters. *Contract Recruiter.*

4. Flowers, V. S., and Hughes, C. L. (1973, July). Why employees stay. *Harvard Business Review.*

5. Seppala, E., and King, M. (2017, August 8). Having work friends can be tricky, but it's worth it. *Harvard Business Review.*

6. Mejia, Z. (2018, March 30). Why having friends at work is so crucial for your success. *CNBC.*

7. Cutter, C. (2022, June 25). Bosses swear by the 90-day rule to keep workers long term. *Wall Street Journal.*

8. Cutter, C. (2022, June 25). Bosses swear by the 90-day rule to keep workers long term. *Wall Street Journal.*

Chapter 3

1. Eichenwald, K. (2012, July 3). Microsoft's lost decade. *Vanity Fair.*

2. Buckingham, M., and Goodall, A. (2015, April). Reinventing performance management. *Harvard Business Review.*

3. Cunningham, L. (2015, July 23). Accenture CEO explains why he's overhauling performance reviews. *The Washington Post.*

4. Sutton, R., and Wigert, B. (2019, May 6). More harm than good: The truth about performance reviews. *Gallup Workplace*.

5. Scott, K. (2019). *Radical Candor. How to Get What You Want by Saying What You Mean*. New York, NY: St. Martin's Press.

6. Scott, K. (2019). *Radical Candor: Be a Kick-Ass Boss Without Losing Your Humanity*. New York, NY: St. Martin's Press.

7. The phrase "feedback sandwich" is most commonly attributed to Mary Kay Ash, the founder of Mary Kay Cosmetics.

8. Farragher, T., and Nelson, S. (2002, October 24). Business record helps, hinders Romney. *Boston Globe*.

9. Robison, J. (2006, November 9). In praise of praising your employees. *Gallup Workplace*.

Chapter 4

1. Fleenor, J., and Prince, J. (1997). *Using 360-Degree Feedback in Organizations*. Greensboro, NC: Center for Creative Leadership.

2. Zenger, J., and Folkman, J. (2012, September 7). Getting 360 degree reviews right. *Harvard Business Review*.

3. Because of the sensitive nature of the case, the names have been fictionalized, as has been the exact feedback provided. However, the tone and general content is true to the actual situation.

4. Marcroft, D. (2021 June 22). *A silenced workforce: Four in five employees feel colleagues aren't heard equally* [online]. UKG.

Chapter 5

1. Eagle Hill Consulting. (2015). *Are low performers destroying your culture and driving away your best employees? Here's what you can do* [online].

2. Some feel that everyone needs to be an A-player. I find this to be aspirational. Most organizations have positions where a B-player is acceptable, and the time and energy (and expense) in replacing that person with an A-player interferes with more important priorities. I recommend putting maximum energy into those high-impact positions where the difference between a B and an A will have the strongest impact on your organization.

3. I credit Graham Weaver for the simple and useful tool of adding the three words "in three years" in front of many questions, especially those related to personnel.

4. These questions were co-developed with my Stanford colleague, Graham Weaver.

5. Manzoni, J-F., and Barsoux, J-L. (1998, March–April). The set-up-to-fail syndrome, *Harvard Business Review*.

6. Sutton, R. (2007). *The No Asshole Rule: Building a Civilized Workplace and Surviving One That Isn't*. New York, NY: Hachette Book Group.

7. Insults, violation of personal space, unsolicited touching, threats, sarcasm, flames, humiliation, shaming, interruption, backbiting, glaring, and snubbing.

8. Collins, J. (2001). *Good to Great: Why Some Companies Make the Leap . . . and Others Don't*. New York, NY: Harper Business.

9. I have been unable to find out who originally said the first version of this expression. Dave Thomas popularized it in a 2007 Qcon talk, but I have found earlier references to the same expression.

Chapter 6

1. Axelrod, B., Handfield-Jones, H., and Michaels, E. (2002, January). A new game plan for C players. *Harvard Business Review*.

2. Dalio, R. Bridgewater Associates.

3. Employee benefits such as COBRA are subject to change. COBRA is described only to illustrate the broader concept that you should carefully review with experts in your jurisdiction and industry the laws and regulations that may apply, and to be well prepared when you meet with the impacted employee.

4. This has been my experience with employment litigation. This experience does not necessarily apply to your situation, and you should consult your attorney and advisors before deciding on your case, facts, and circumstances.

5. If you have any reason to believe someone may become violent or create a dangerous situation for your team, carefully consult with experts prior to your meeting. If you are in any doubt or feel you could benefit from additional experience, get expert advice.

6. Peterson, J. (2020, March-April). Firing with compassion. *Harvard Business Review*.

Chapter 7

1. McFeely, S., and Wigert, B. (2019, March 13). This fixable problem cost U.S. businesses $1 trillion [online]. *Gallup Workplace*.

2. Ibid.

3. Ibid.

4. Nelson, N. (2021). *Make More Money by Making Your Employees Happy*. 2nd ed.

5. Brooks, A. (2022, October 13). If you want success, pursue happiness. *The Atlantic*.

6. Ken Blanchard is often credited with coining the phrase, although he gives credit to his partner Rick Tate, who worked with Blanchard at The Ken Blanchard Companies, an international management training and consulting firm founded in 1979.

Chapter 8

1. Similar work on time and motion was also undertaken by Fredrick Taylor.

2. Sutton, R., and Rao, H. (2014). *Scaling Up Excellence: Getting to More Without Settling for Less.* New York, NY: Crown Business Books.

3. EarthDate. (2020). *How 10 fingers became 12 hours* [online].

4. Porter, M., and Nohria, N. (2018, July–August). How CEOs manage time. *Harvard Business Review.*

5. Mark, G. (2006, June 8). Too many interruptions at work? *Gallup Business Journal.*

6. Gehl, K., and Porter, M. (2020). *The Politics Industry: How Political Innovation Can Break Partisan Gridlock and Save Our Democracy.* Boston, MA: Harvard Business Review Press.

7. Newport, C. (2016). *Deep Work: Rules for Focused Success in a Distracted World.* New York, NY: Grant Central Publishing.

8. Perlow, L. (1999). The time famine: Toward a sociology of work time. *Administrative, Science Quarterly, 44*(1).

9. Horne, J. A., and Östberg, O. (1976). A self-assessment questionnaire to determine morningness-eveningness in human circadian rhythms. *International Journal of Chronobiology, 4*(2).

10. Fogg, B. J. (2020). *Tiny Habits: The Small Changes That Change Everything.* Boston, MA: Mariner Books.

Chapter 9

1. Lewis, N. A., and Oyserman, D. (2015, April 23). When does the future begin? Time metrics matter, connecting present and future selves *Psychological Science, 26*(6).

2. Parker, J. (2021, June 18). An ode to procrastination. *The Atlantic.*

3. Techonomy Media. (2011). *Jack Dorsey on working for two companies full-time* [Video]. YouTube.

4. McTighe, J., and Willis, J. (2019). *Upgrade Your Teaching: Understanding by Design Meets Neuroscience.* Alexandria, VA: ASCD.

Chapter 10

1. Mankins, M., Brahm, C., and Caimi, G. (2014, May). Your scarcest resource. *Harvard Business Review.*

2. 2019 Adobe Email Usage Study.

3. De Semet, A., Hewes, C., Luo, M., Maxwell, J. R., and Simon, P. (2022, January 10). *If we're all so busy, why isn't anything getting done?* [online] McKinsey & Company.

4. Porter, M., and Nohria, N. (2018, July–August). How CEOs manage their time. *Harvard Business Review.*

5. Stone, Lisa. Founder, The Attention Project.

6. Jackson, T., Dawson, R., and Wilson, D. (2003). *Understanding email interaction increases organizational productivity* [online]. Loughborough University.

7. Peck, S. (2019, September 20). 6 ways to set boundaries around email. *Harvard Business Review.*

8. Jackson, T., Dawson, R., and Wilson, D. (2003). *Understanding email interaction increases organizational productivity* [online]. Loughborough University.

9. Leswig, K. (2016, April 18). The average iPhone is unlocked 80 times per day. *Business Insider.*

10. Statista (2022). *Daily time spent on social networking by internet users worldwide from 2012 to 2022* [online].

11. Marshall, J. (2021, April 2). Scale was the god that failed. *The Atlantic.*

12. Dabbish, L., Kraut, R., Fussell S., and Kiesler, S. (2005, April). *Understanding Email Use: Predicting Action on a Message. Human-Computer Interaction Institute.* School of Computer Science, Carnegie Mellon University.

13. Plummer, M. (2019, January 22). How to spend way less time on email every day. *Harvard Business Review.*

14. Mankins, M., Brahm, C., and Caimi, G. (2014, May). Your scarcest resource. *Harvard Business Review.*

Chapter 11

1. Bonsall, A. (2022, September 29). 3 types of meetings—and how to do each one well. *Harvard Business Review.*

2. Mankins, M., Brahm, C., and Caimi, G. (2014, May). Your scarcest resource. *Harvard Business Review.*

3. Ibid.

4. Rogelberg, S., Scott, C., and Kello, J. (2007). The science and fiction of meetings. *MIT Sloan Management Review, 48*(2).

5. De Semet, A., Hewes, C., Luo, M., Maxwell, J. R., and Simon, P. (2022, January 10). *If we're all so busy, why isn't anything getting done?* [online]. McKinsey & Company.

6. Kennedy, R. (1971). *Thirteen days: A Memoir of the Cuban Missile Crisis.* New York, NY: W.W. Norton & Company.

7. Baer, D., and De Luce, I. (2019, August 13). 11 Tricks Steve Jobs, Jeff Bezos, and other famous execs use to run meetings. *Business Insider.*

8. A view generally attributed to former US Senator Daniel Patrick Moynihan.

9. Drucker, P. (2004, June). What makes an effective executive. *Harvard Business Review.*

Chapter 12

1. When we teach a case in business school, while the general situation is described accurately, some of the facts and names are adjusted to increase the learning potential of the situation, as well as preserve confidentiality. This is the situation with the case on Dulbecco and Torani.

Chapter 13

1. Some organizations require their employees to enter into confidentiality agreements, which may limit what can be told to others. You'll want to be mindful not to do anything that may encourage someone to knowingly, or unknowingly, violate the terms of any such agreement.

2. Cohen, B. (2022, October 20). What happened when the U.S. military played "Shark Tank." *Wall Street Journal*.

Chapter 14

1. Barra, M. (2015, August 3). *My mentors told me to take an HR role even though I was an engineer. They were right* [online]. LinkedIn.

2. Zalta, E. N., and Nodelman, U. (Eds.). (2022). *The Stanford Encyclopedia of Philosophy* [online]. Stanford University.

3. Bridges, T. (2014, January–February). Elway rallies again. *Stanford Magazine*, Stanford, California.

Chapter 15

1. Symonds, M. (2011, January 21). Executive coaching—another set of clothes for the emperor? *Forbes*.

2. Schmidt, E., Rosenberg, J., and Eagle, A. (2019). *Trillion Dollar Coach: The Leadership Playbook of Silicon Valley's Bill Campbell*. New York, NY: HarperCollins.

3. Freeman, M., Johnson, S., Staudenmaier, P., and Zisser, M. (2015). *Are Entrepreneurs "Touched with Fire"?* The University of California and Stanford University.

4. Larker, D., Miles S., Tayan, B., and Gutman, M. (2013). *2013 Executive Coaching Survey.* The Miles Group and Stanford University.

5. Symonds, M. (2011, January 21). Executive coaching – another set of clothes for the emperor? *Forbes.*

Chapter 17

1. Porter, M., and Nohria, N. (2018, July–August). How CEOs manage time. *Harvard Business Review.*

2. I credit Joel Peterson, my colleague at Stanford and a founding investor of Jet Blue, for the expression of flying at the right altitude.

3. Ittner, C., and Larcker, D. (2003, November). Coming up short on nonfinancial performance measurement. *Harvard Business Review.*

4. I am using a rudamentary definition of standard deviation to make the critical point about simplicity. The more accurate definition of standard deviation is the dispersion of data as compared to the mathematical mean.

5. Southwest Airlines. (2021). *A turning point: The birth of the 10-mintue turn* [online].

Chapter 18

1. I owe a debt to Jeff Stevens, among other things founder of Anacapa Partners, who years ago first introduced me to the concept of a baseline budget.

2. Isaacson, W. (2012, April). The real leadership lessons of Steve Jobs. *Harvard Business Review.*

3. Bariso, J. (2019). Bill Gates, Warren Buffett, and Steve Jobs all used one word to their advantage—and it led to amazing success. *Inc.*

4. Schwantes, M. (2022). Warren Buffett says what separates successful people from everyone else really comes down to a two-letter word. *Inc.*

5. Heath, C., and Heath, D. (2011). *Switch: How to Change Things When Change Is Hard.* Waterville, ME: Thorndike Press.

Chapter 19

1. Hays Recruiting Specialists. (2017, October 16). *What People Want Report.*

2. While associated primarily with Drucker and his immensely influential book, *The Practice of Management,* it was first used by George T. Doran: Doran, G. T. (1981). There's a SMART way to write management's goals and objectives. *Management Review.*

3. July/August Conference Board Review.

4. The concept and name, Night on the Town, originally came from Tandem Computers, which eventually became part of Hewlett-Packard. My understanding is that it was a program created by Jimmy Treybig, the founder of Tandem Computers.

5. Sutton, R., and Rao, H. (2014). *Scaling Up Excellence: Getting to More Without Settling for Less.* New York, NY: Crown Business.

6. There are payroll tax implications of offering compensation in the form of cash, which need to be understood and considered when paying employees in cash.

Chapter 20

1. Gates, B. (1999). *Business @ the Speed of Thought.* New York, NY: Warner Books.

2. Debruyne, F., and Dullweber, A. (2015, April 8). *The five disciplines of customer experience leaders* [online]. Bain & Company Insights.

3. Afshar, V. (2017, December 6). 50 important customer experience stats for business leaders. *Huffington Post*. Based on work by Kolsky, E. (2017). *thinkJar annual survey*.

4. Hyken, S. (2020, July 12). Ninety-six percent of customers will leave you for bad customer service. *Forbes*.

5. Roesler, P. (2017, December 18). American Express study shows rising consumer expectations for good customer service. *Inc*.

6. Dolan, R. (1995, September–October). How do you know when the price is right? *Harvard Business Review*.

7. Ibid.

8. Popularized in 1956 by Dr. Armand Feigenbaum, MIT Sloan School of Management.

9. Taguchi, G., and Clausing, D. (1990, January–February). Robust Quality. *Harvard Business Review*.

10. Dimensional Research. (2013, April). *Customer service and business results: A survey of customer service from mid-size companies* [online].

Chapter 21

1. Svenson, O. (1981). Are we all less risky and more skillful than our fellow drivers? *Acta Psychologica, 47*(2).

2. Schwager, A., and Meyer, C. (2007, February). Understanding customer experience. *Harvard Business Review*.

3. Net promoter score: A scale of 1 to 10 ("not at all likely" to "extremely likely") that asks of their probability of recommending a particular product or service to a friend or colleague. NPS has been demonstrated to be an indicator of customer satisfaction.

4. Dixon, M., Freeman, K., and Toman, N. (2010, July–August). Stop trying to delight your customers. *Harvard Business Review*.

5. Aral, S. (2013, December 19). The problem with online ratings. *MIT Sloan Management Review*; Klein, N. et al. (2018, March 6). Online reviews are biased. Here's how to fix them. *Harvard Business Review*.

6. Mauboussin, M. (2012, October). The true measures of success. *Harvard Business Review*.

7. Kosur, J. (2015, December 16). Intuit's CFO wants to follow you home and watch you work. *Business Insider*.

8. Solomon, M. (2018, December 23). How Safelite built a customer service culture, doubled revenue by consulting customers directly. *Forbes*.

9. Net promoter score (NPS): A scale of 1 to 10 ("not at all likely" to "extremely likely") that asks of their probability of recommending your product or service to a friend or colleague.

10. Customer effort score (CES): A scale, generally from 1–5, that uses survey tools to ask users to rate the ease or difficulty of their customer experience. CES is generally surveyed immediately after an interaction, with a simple question such as "Dave's Donuts made it easy to get my donut," followed by a scale where 1 is "strongly disagree" and 5 is "strongly agree."

11. First contact resolution (FCR): A percentage measurement of how frequently a customer's issue is resolved at the first point of contact. FCR is generally compiled internally based on information provided by the company versus the customer.

12. Customer satisfaction (CSAT): A scale, generally from 1–5, that uses survey tools to ask users to rate the overall satisfaction of their customer experience. CSAT is generally surveyed with a simple question such as "How would you rate your overall satisfaction with your donut today?" followed by a scale where 1 is "very unsatisfied" and 5 is "very satisfied."

13. Debruyne, F., and Dullweber, A. (2015, April 8). *The five disciplines of customer experience leaders*. Bain & Company Insights.

Chapter 22

1. Shults, T. (2019, August 1). Comeback story: A new chapter for indie bookstores. *The Christian Science Monitor.*

2. Raffaelli, R. (2020). Reinventing retail: The novel resurgence of independent bookstores (Working Paper 20-068). Cambridge, MA: Harvard Business School.

3. Hahn, F. (2019, February 21). How do indie bookstores compete with Amazon? Personality—and a sense of community. *The Washington Post.*

4. Debruyne, F., and Dullweber, A. (2015, April 8). *The five disciplines of customer experience leaders.* Bain & Company Insights.

5. Ibid.

6. Fortune (2011). 100 best companies to work for. *CNN Money.*

7. Todorov, G. (2021, March 22). *Word of Mouth Marketing: 49 Statistics to Help You Boost Your Bottom Line.* Boston, MA: Semrush.

8. Celso, A., Henrique, J. L., and Rossi, C. (2007, August). Service recovery paradox: A meta-analysis. *Journal of Service Research, 10*(1).

9. A second reason for adding greeters was to reduce shoplifting.

10. Dusharme, D. (n.d.). Six Sigma survey: Breaking through the Six Sigma hype. *Quality Digest.*

11. Takeuchi, H., and Quelch, J. (1983, July). Quality is more than making a good product. *Harvard Business Magazine.*

12. The example of a shooting range was inspired by Genichi Taguchi and Don Clausing, who made a similar point in a January–February 1990 article published in the *Harvard Business Review,* titled Robust Quality.

13. At a former company I ran in New England, Wind River Environmental, this is how we answered the phone. However, I first heard the phrase from Dalworth Carpets, which operated an outstanding carpet-cleaning service in Texas and served as a quality mentor to me early in my career.

INDEX